DINOSAURS EYE TO EYE

Zoom in on the world's most incredible dinosaurs

**LONDON, NEW YORK, MUNICH,
MELBOURNE, AND DELHI**

Senior editor Shaila Brown
Senior art editor Philip Letsu
Art editor Johnny Pau
Managing editor Linda Esposito
Managing art editor Diane Thistlethwaite
Publishing manager Andrew Macintyre
Category publisher Laura Buller
Picture researcher Myriam Megharbi
DK picture library Emma Shepherd
Cartographer Ed Merrit
Creative technical support Peter Pawsey
Production editor Melissa Latorre
Production controller Charlotte Oliver
Jacket editor Joanna Pocock
Jacket designer Laura Brim
Jacket manager Sophia M. Tampakopoulos Turner
Creative retouching Steve Willis

Consultant Dr. Darren Naish

First published in the United States in 2010 by
DK Publishing Inc., 375 Hudson Street, New York, New York 10014

A Penguin Company
Copyright © 2010 Dorling Kindersley Limited
09 10 11 12 13 10 9 8 7 6 5 4 3 2 1
DD532— 01/10

DK books are available at special discounts when purchased in bulk
for sales promotions, premiums, fundraising, or educational use.
For details, contact: DK Publishing Special Markets,
375 Hudson Street, New York, New York 10014
SpecialSales@dk.com

A catalog record for this book is
available from the Library of Congress.

ISBN 978-0-7566-5760-4

Color reproduction by MDP, United Kingdom
Printed by Star Standard, Singapore

Discover more at
www.dk.com

DINOSAURS EYE TO EYE

Zoom in on the world's most incredible dinosaurs

Author
John Woodward

Digital Sculptor
Peter Minister

Contents

Fast Facts: the length or wingspan of each prehistoric animal is indicated in comparison to human dimensions – 6 ft (1.8 m).

Dinosaur timeline

The age of dinosaurs began some 230 million years ago, near the beginning of the Mesozoic era. Dinosaurs went on to dominate life on Earth for 165 million years—a vast span of time that permitted the evolution of a dazzling variety of species. They were fantastically successful animals, and many were among the biggest and most spectacular creatures that have ever existed. Until recently, we thought they were all extinct—wiped out by some catastrophe 65 million years ago, and surviving only as fossils. Yet we now realize that one group of dinosaurs—birds—still flourishes, so the age of dinosaurs has not ended. We live in it.

Acanthostega was one of the first amphibians.

Ancestors
The earliest land vertebrates appeared roughly 370 million years ago. They were amphibians, which have to live and breed in or near water. Within 80 million years some developed waterproof skins that enabled them to live in dry places. These early reptiles were the ancestors of dinosaurs.

Contemporaries
When dinosaurs appeared in the Triassic period, they were greatly outnumbered by other reptiles known as the crurotarsans. These included powerful animals like *Postosuchus*—a massive-jawed predator that may have preyed on early dinosaurs. During the Mesozoic era, dinosaurs lived alongside flying pterosaurs, marine reptiles, lizards, tortoises, and early mammals.

ERA	MESOZOIC	
PERIOD	Triassic	Jurassic

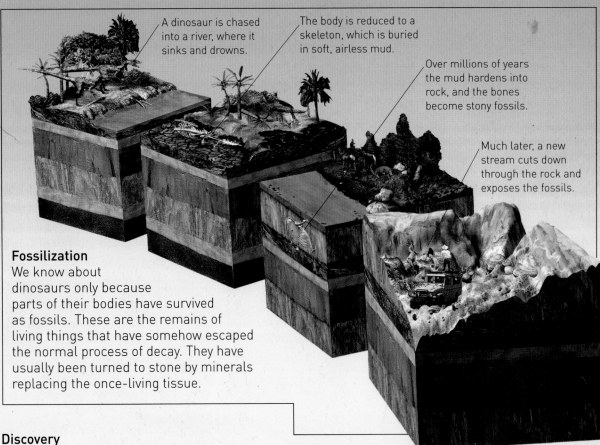

A dinosaur is chased into a river, where it sinks and drowns.

The body is reduced to a skeleton, which is buried in soft, airless mud.

Over millions of years the mud hardens into rock, and the bones become stony fossils.

Much later, a new stream cuts down through the rock and exposes the fossils.

Fossilization

We know about dinosaurs only because parts of their bodies have survived as fossils. These are the remains of living things that have somehow escaped the normal process of decay. They have usually been turned to stone by minerals replacing the once-living tissue.

Discovery

Most dinosaur fossils consist of bones and teeth, which fossilize well because they survive decay long enough to be buried in sediments that turn to rock. But other fossils include skin, feathers, and even a last meal! When such fossils are exposed by erosion, they often have to be chipped out of the rock. Small skeletons are left attached to the slab, but bigger bones, like the ones shown here, are carefully removed when their positions have been fully and accurately recorded.

Catastrophe

The Mesozoic era ended 65 million years ago in a mass extinction that wiped out many types of animals and plants. Scientists are not sure what caused this catastrophe. An asteroid impact in what is now Mexico may have caused a huge explosion followed by years of acid rain and climate chaos. Massive volcanic eruptions in what is now India may have had a similar effect. Either way, the disaster eliminated all dinosaurs except birds. Other reptiles also survived, as did amphibians and mammals.

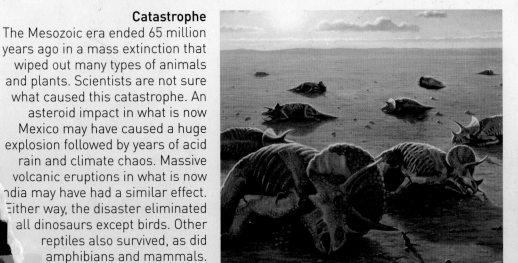

Reconstruction

Once the bones are conserved, they can be used to make lightweight copies for assembly into mounted skeletons. This worker is welding a steel framework for a *Barosaurus*. The bones reveal a lot about the animal, enabling scientists to reconstruct its likely appearance when alive.

Timeline

The Mesozoic era consisted of the Triassic, Jurassic, and Cretaceous periods. This age of giant dinosaurs lasted much longer than the Cenozoic era that followed, and 40 times as long as anything resembling humanity, which appeared near the end of the Neogene period.

CENOZOIC

Cretaceous

Paleogene

Neogene

What is a dinosaur?

We often think of dinosaurs as huge land-living reptiles that vanished off the face of Earth many millions of years ago. Yet while some dinosaurs were certainly giants, others were relatively small, nimble creatures. One group even took to the air, and they still survive as birds. So our old image of dinosaurs as lumbering prehistoric monsters has dramatically changed. They were not like most of the cold-blooded reptiles we know today, but dynamic, probably warm-blooded creatures with distinctive anatomical features. The same could be said for the closely related pterosaurs that flew in the Mesozoic skies and evolved into the most spectacular flying animals of all time.

Reptiles with a difference
Dinosaurs were reptiles—part of a group that includes tortoises, crocodiles, and lizards. All of these animals evolved from a shared ancestor that was almost certainly cold-blooded and scaly, like this lizard. But Mesozoic dinosaurs were probably warm-blooded, and many had feathers like modern birds. They were reptiles, but reptiles with a difference.

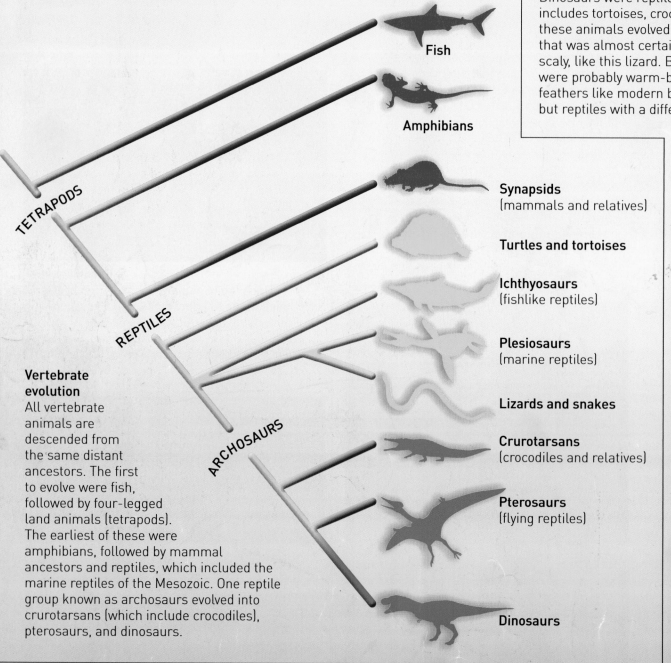

Fish

Amphibians

TETRAPODS

REPTILES

ARCHOSAURS

Synapsids
(mammals and relatives)

Turtles and tortoises

Ichthyosaurs
(fishlike reptiles)

Plesiosaurs
(marine reptiles)

Lizards and snakes

Crurotarsans
(crocodiles and relatives)

Pterosaurs
(flying reptiles)

Dinosaurs

Vertebrate evolution
All vertebrate animals are descended from the same distant ancestors. The first to evolve were fish, followed by four-legged land animals (tetrapods). The earliest of these were amphibians, followed by mammal ancestors and reptiles, which included the marine reptiles of the Mesozoic. One reptile group known as archosaurs evolved into crurotarsans (which include crocodiles), pterosaurs, and dinosaurs.

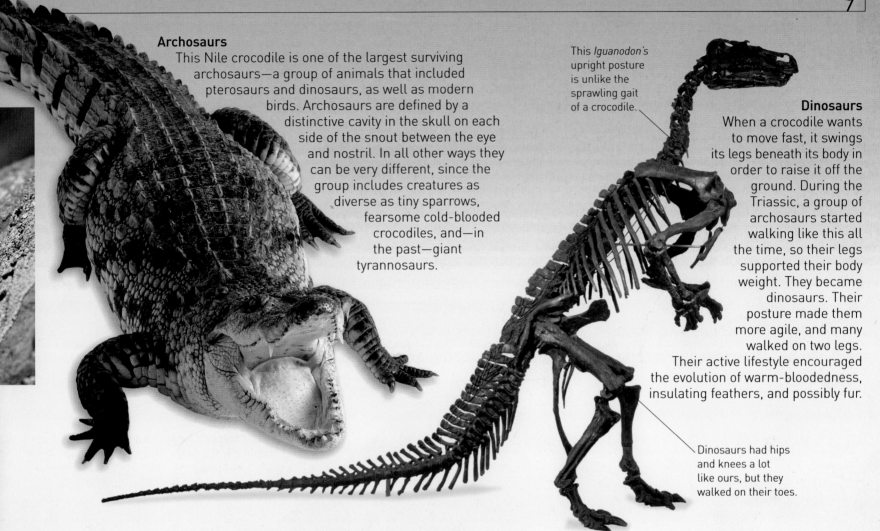

Archosaurs

This Nile crocodile is one of the largest surviving archosaurs—a group of animals that included pterosaurs and dinosaurs, as well as modern birds. Archosaurs are defined by a distinctive cavity in the skull on each side of the snout between the eye and nostril. In all other ways they can be very different, since the group includes creatures as diverse as tiny sparrows, fearsome cold-blooded crocodiles, and—in the past—giant tyrannosaurs.

This *Iguanodon's* upright posture is unlike the sprawling gait of a crocodile.

Dinosaurs

When a crocodile wants to move fast, it swings its legs beneath its body in order to raise it off the ground. During the Triassic, a group of archosaurs started walking like this all the time, so their legs supported their body weight. They became dinosaurs. Their posture made them more agile, and many walked on two legs. Their active lifestyle encouraged the evolution of warm-bloodedness, insulating feathers, and possibly fur.

Dinosaurs had hips and knees a lot like ours, but they walked on their toes.

Pterosaurs

One early group of archosaurs took to the air: pterosaurs. They had furry bodies and batlike wings made of skin reinforced with stiff fibers and muscles, supported by the bones of a single long finger. They had big flight muscles and flew well. But many, such as this *Pterodactylus*, also hunted on the ground.

Marine reptiles

Although they were not archosaurs and so not very closely related to dinosaurs, the Mesozoic marine reptiles were spectacular animals. Some, such as this *Mosasaurus*, were huge, powerful predators. Like the pterosaurs, they vanished at the end of the Mesozoic era.

Types of dinosaurs

Thousands of dinosaurs evolved during the Mesozoic era. We have found the remains of only a fraction of them, so scientists can never be sure that they have identified every main type. Yet the evidence shows that all dinosaurs except the earliest ones belonged to two groups—saurischians and ornithischians. These terms refer to the basic structure of their pelvic bones, but they were also distinguished by other features. For example, saurischians had longer, more flexible necks, and ornithischians had beaks supported by special jawbones. The saurischians evolved into the mostly meat-eating theropods and the plant-eating sauropodomorphs. The ornithischians split into three main types, almost all plant eaters.

Some sauropods had longer necks than any animals that have ever lived. The neck bones of *Brachiosaurus* were each up to 3 ft (1 m) long.

Sauropodomorphs
The sauropodomorphs included the biggest of all dinosaurs—huge sauropods like *Brachiosaurus*. They were all plant eaters that needed big, heavy digestive systems. Their ancestors walked on their hind legs, but the giant sauropods supported their immense weight on four feet.

Family tree
This diagram shows the five main groups of dinosaurs. The theropods were mostly hunters such as the fearsome *Tyrannosaurus rex*. The sauropodomorphs included the huge, long-necked plant-eating sauropods. The thyreophorans consisted of the stegosaurs and armored ankylosaurs. These evolved before the ornithopods and marginocephalians, which included both horned ceratopsians and the pachycephalosaurs, or bone heads.

Saurischian dinosaurs had forward-pointing pubis bones in the pelvis. But later, some saurischians evolved their own version of the ornithischian-type pelvis.

DINOSAURS

All ornithischian dinosaurs had backward-pointing pubis bones in the pelvis. This allowed the heavy digestive system of a plant eater to lie farther back, so the animal's center of gravity was closer to its hind legs.

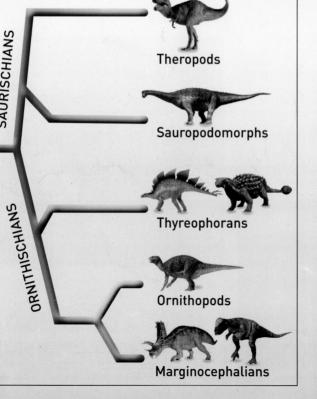

SAURISCHIANS

Theropods

Sauropodomorphs

ORNITHISCHIANS

Thyreophorans

Ornithopods

Marginocephalians

Many theropods had small front limbs, but those of tyrannosaurids were tiny.

Theropods
The theropods all walked on their hind legs, and almost all of them were hunters. Some were powerful giants like this *Albertosaurus*. Others, such as *Velociraptor*, were smaller and more agile. Many had feathers, and one group of these that developed the ability to fly still survives—they are birds.

Thyreophorans

In the Early Jurassic era, one branch of the ornithischian line evolved into the thyreophorans. There were two groups of these: stegosaurs like *Kentrosaurus*, with its long spines and dorsal plates, and the heavily armored ankylosaurs. The stegosaurs were mostly Jurassic, but ankylosaurs flourished during the Cretaceous.

Ornithopods

The ornithopods were one of the most successful groups of ornithischians. They were plant eaters, like the sauropods, but their pelvic structure allowed their heavy intestines to lie farther back in the body. This enabled many to walk upright, but bigger ones such as this *Iguanodon* often stood on four legs. They had chewing teeth, and like all ornithischians, they had short beaks.

With longer front legs than other sauropods, *Brachiosaurus* was very tall at the shoulder.

The huge body contained a bulky digestive system that fermented the animal's leafy food to extract the nutrients.

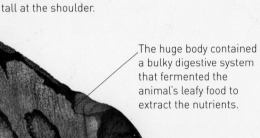

Immensely strong pillarlike legs resembling those of an outsize elephant supported the dinosaur's colossal weight.

Marginocephalians

The last group of dinosaurs to appear were the marginocephalians. These included horned dinosaurs, or ceratopsians, like this *Einiosaurus* and the pachycephalosaurs with their extra-thick "bone head" skulls. The horns and frills of these animals were probably mostly ornamental.

Triassic world

The first dinosaurs appeared roughly halfway through the first period of the Mesozoic era—the Triassic, which lasted from 251 to 199 million years ago. The previous era—the Paleozoic—had ended in a catastrophic mass extinction that destroyed at least 90 percent of all known living species. The surviving animals evolved into new forms that could take advantage of the conditions. Eventually, some 15 million years after the great extinction, this process gave rise to the dinosaurs. They took time to get into their stride, however, and did not start to dominate life on land until the Late Triassic, possibly because smaller extinction events had wiped out many of their competitors.

Supercontinent

The continents are in constant, very slow motion as they are carried around the globe by the mobile plates of Earth's crust. In the Early Triassic, they had pushed together to form a supercontinent called Pangaea, surrounded by the Panthalassic Ocean. Pangaea started to break in two during the Late Triassic as the Tethys Ocean opened up.

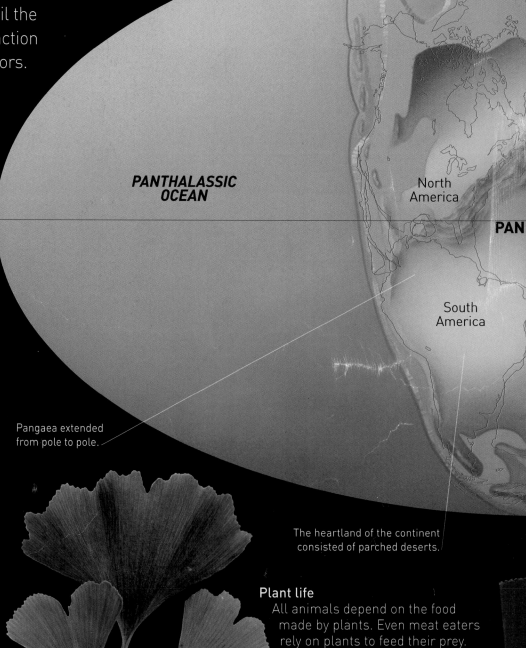

PANTHALASSIC
OCEAN

North
America

PAN

South
America

Pangaea extended
from pole to pole.

The heartland of the continent
consisted of parched deserts.

Ginkgo
leaves

Climate

Large areas of land at the heart of Pangaea were a long way from the ocean. As a result, they got very little rainfall and were hot, arid deserts. Most of the plants and animals lived near the edges of the continent, where the influence of the ocean made the climate cooler and wetter.

Plant life

All animals depend on the food made by plants. Even meat eaters rely on plants to feed their prey. During the Triassic, the main edible plants were primitive types such as clubmosses, horsetails, and ferns, as well as conifer trees, ginkgos, and palmlike cycads. There were no grasses or flowering plants.

Insects and spiders

Although the mass extinction at the end of the Paleozoic destroyed a lot of animal life, many insects, spiders, and other invertebrates survived. They included creatures like this fossilized dragonfly. Over time, they flourished and evolved new forms, providing food for larger animals such as reptiles.

Thecodontosaurus was a primitive plant eater.

Green and yellow indicate the area of land above sea level during the Triassic.

Siberia

Europe

North China

South China

Turkey

GAEA

Iran

Indochina

Tibet

Malay Peninsula

Africa Arabia

TETHYS OCEAN

India

Australia

Antarctica

Red outline indicates how the Triassic continents split up to become today's continents or landmasses.

Dinosaurs

Dinosaurs evolved from a group of reptiles called the archosaurs, which also included a variety of crocodilelike creatures. The first dinosaurs were quite small compared to later ones, walked mostly on their hind legs, and ate a variety of foods. By the Late Triassic, such "all-purpose" dinosaurs, like this *Thecodontosaurus*, were evolving into more specialized hunters and plant eaters.

Placerias

Mammal ancestors

For most of the Triassic, dinosaurs were outnumbered by other animals such as lizards, tortoises, crocodilians, and mammal ancestors like *Placerias*. This hippolike plant eater was one of the last survivors of a group of animals that faded as dinosaurs began to flourish—but not before giving rise to the first mammals.

Life in the water

Despite the mass extinction that ended the Paleozoic era, enough animals survived in the Triassic oceans to evolve into a wonderful variety of marine life. They included invertebrates, fish, and placodonts such as *Henodus*—an armored reptile that fed mostly on shellfish.

The head was long and flat. It was a lot like the head of a modern crocodile, primarily adapted for catching fish.

Nothosaurus had a long, flexible, well-muscled neck. This enabled it to throw its head sideways in the water to seize passing fish in its long jaws. This specialized "snap feeding" technique is used today by some crocodiles.

Nothosaurus

In the Middle Triassic, when dinosaurs were just beginning to appear on land, the main oceanic fish hunters were nothosaurs like *Nothosaurus*. They were relatives of the plesiosaurs but less aquatic. *Nothosaurus* fossils occur on sites that were once the northern shores of the ancient Tethys Ocean, where the animals probably hunted in shallow coastal waters.

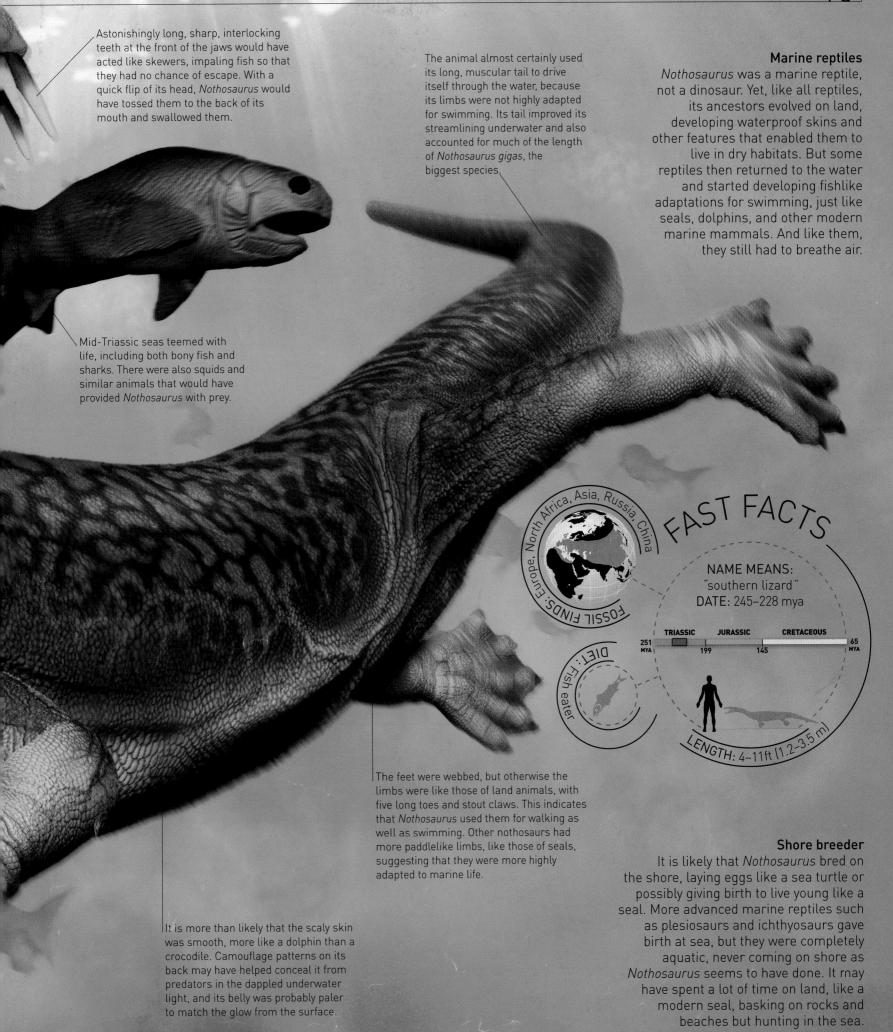

Astonishingly long, sharp, interlocking teeth at the front of the jaws would have acted like skewers, impaling fish so that they had no chance of escape. With a quick flip of its head, *Nothosaurus* would have tossed them to the back of its mouth and swallowed them.

The animal almost certainly used its long, muscular tail to drive itself through the water, because its limbs were not highly adapted for swimming. Its tail improved its streamlining underwater and also accounted for much of the length of *Nothosaurus gigas*, the biggest species.

Marine reptiles

Nothosaurus was a marine reptile, not a dinosaur. Yet, like all reptiles, its ancestors evolved on land, developing waterproof skins and other features that enabled them to live in dry habitats. But some reptiles then returned to the water and started developing fishlike adaptations for swimming, just like seals, dolphins, and other modern marine mammals. And like them, they still had to breathe air.

Mid-Triassic seas teemed with life, including both bony fish and sharks. There were also squids and similar animals that would have provided *Nothosaurus* with prey.

FAST FACTS

FOSSIL FINDS: Europe, North Africa, Asia, Russia, China

DIET: Fish eater

NAME MEANS: "southern lizard"
DATE: 245–228 mya

TRIASSIC	JURASSIC	CRETACEOUS
251 MYA	199	145	65 MYA

LENGTH: 4–11ft (1.2–3.5 m)

The feet were webbed, but otherwise the limbs were like those of land animals, with five long toes and stout claws. This indicates that *Nothosaurus* used them for walking as well as swimming. Other nothosaurs had more paddlelike limbs, like those of seals, suggesting that they were more highly adapted to marine life.

Shore breeder

It is likely that *Nothosaurus* bred on the shore, laying eggs like a sea turtle or possibly giving birth to live young like a seal. More advanced marine reptiles such as plesiosaurs and ichthyosaurs gave birth at sea, but they were completely aquatic, never coming on shore as *Nothosaurus* seems to have done. It may have spent a lot of time on land, like a modern seal, basking on rocks and beaches but hunting in the sea.

It is more than likely that the scaly skin was smooth, more like a dolphin than a crocodile. Camouflage patterns on its back may have helped conceal it from predators in the dappled underwater light, and its belly was probably paler to match the glow from the surface.

Most of *Eoraptor*'s teeth were like serrated blades, ideal for slicing through meat. The theropods that evolved later had these, too, but so did many other meat-eating reptiles, so they do not indicate that *Eoraptor* was a theropod. However, it was certainly a hunter.

Eoraptor

This agile fox-size animal was one of the first dinosaurs. Its sharp teeth and claws indicate that it was a hunter, and it probably chased lizards and other small animals through the Late Triassic undergrowth of what is now South America. Like most early dinosaurs, *Eoraptor* ran on its hind legs—four-footed forms evolved later—so apart from its size it looks a lot like one of the big meat-eating theropods that were the top predators of the Mesozoic era.

Although long and bristling with teeth, the lower jaw was not very deep and strong. The animal would not have had a very powerful bite, and it probably preyed mostly on small reptiles and the early shrewlike mammals that were just beginning to evolve in the Late Triassic.

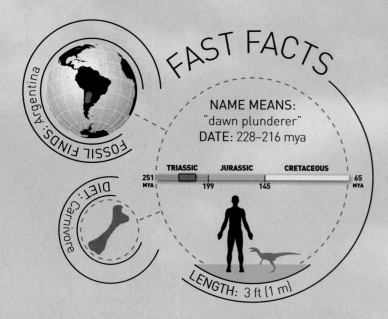

FAST FACTS

FOSSIL FINDS: Argentina

DIET: Carnivore

NAME MEANS:
"dawn plunderer"
DATE: 228–216 mya

TRIASSIC	JURASSIC	CRETACEOUS

251 MYA   199   145   65 MYA

LENGTH: 3 ft (1 m)

The eyes faced mostly to the side, so the animal's stereoscopic vision was quite limited. *Eoraptor* did have a good all-around view, however—vital for a small animal at risk from more powerful predators like the much bigger *Herrerasaurus* that lived in the

Valley of the Moon
The remains of *Eoraptor* have been found in northwestern Argentina, in a region known as the Valley of the Moon. It is named for its barren, almost lunar landscape of sandstones and mudstones, laid down by rivers in the Late Triassic. These are the sediments that contain the *Eoraptor* fossils.

The neck of *Eoraptor* was shorter than the necks of similar but later hunters, but it was still long and flexible. This enabled it to snatch fast-moving prey from the ground and possibly from low-growing plants.

No fossil remains of the skin have been found, so we do not know whether *Eoraptor* had scales or simple feathers. However, we do know that it lived in a region with a warm climate. So, if it was warm-blooded, it would not have needed much insulation.

The hind legs were twice as long as the front ones and much more strongly built, with powerful muscles. This shows that the animal stood upright, balanced by its long tail. This gave it the agility it needed to chase its prey—and escape its enemies.

Primitive dinosaur
When *Eoraptor* was found, it was identified as an early type of theropod—the group that includes almost all the later carnivorous dinosaurs. But recent research shows that it was a more primitive type of dinosaur, stemming from a period before the split between the meat-eating theropods and plant-eating sauropodomorphs. This means that it is one of the earliest of the saurischians and one of the most ancestral of all dinosaurs.

Eoraptor ran on its toes, a lot like a bird. It stood on three of these toes, but it also had another shorter toe that did not reach the ground. This digitigrade (tiptoe) stance is typical of agile, fast-running animals.

Each hand had five fingers, although two were much shorter than the others. Each of the three long fingers had a sharp, sturdy claw that the animal may have used to seize prey and hold it while it got to work with its teeth. But the claws had other uses as well, such as searching vegetation and defending against enemies.

Coelophysis

This slim, lightweight hunter is the best known of a group of small meat-eating dinosaurs that flourished during the Late Triassic and Early Jurassic periods. They were among the earliest theropods—the dinosaurs that were the main predators throughout the Mesozoic era—although their own particular line died out in the Jurassic. *Coelophysis* itself competed for prey with many much bigger, more powerful hunters that were not dinosaurs at all, but giant relatives of crocodilians that dominated life on land during the Triassic.

FOSSIL FINDS: North America, Southern Africa, China

FAST FACTS

NAME MEANS:
"hollow form"
DATE: 228–183 mya

TRIASSIC	JURASSIC	CRETACEOUS

251 MYA

199

145

DIET: Carnivore

LENGTH: 10 ft (3 m)

The skull of *Coelophysis* was long and narrow, with equally long jaws and a shallow jawbone. The jaws were well suited to snapping up small prey but may not have been strong enough for seizing large, powerful animals.

Its long, flexible, mobile neck allowed *Coelophysis* to rapidly dart its head forward to snatch small animals before they had a chance to dive for cover. This was to become a typical feature of all the smaller, more agile theropod hunters of the Mesozoic era.

Although it stood on strong hind legs like all theropods, *Coelophysis* had long front limbs. It had three functional fingers, with stout claws for seizing prey. It also had a very short and probably almost useless fourth finger.

Like most hunters, *Coelophysis* had sharp vision for locating and catching prey. Bones found inside its remains indicate that it hunted small, fast-moving reptiles.

Mass burial

This dinosaur is unusually well known because so many of its skeletons have been found. In 1947, more than 500 *Coelophysis* skeletons were discovered at Ghost Ranch in New Mexico. Most of the animals seem to have died together, possibly because they were drowned by a flash flood. It is likely that they gathered at the site to drink during a drought and were suddenly overwhelmed and buried by a torrent of water and mud.

A long tail helped with balance when running, and its slim build and strong hind legs suggest that *Coelophysis* was quick on its feet. Like all theropods, it had hollow limb bones, saving weight and making it more agile.

Coelophysis had more than 100 small, sharp-pointed teeth in its upper and lower jaws. They were curved, saw-edged blades, ideal for dealing with small prey. It may also have scavenged meat from the carcasses of bigger animals.

Warm-blooded reptiles

Modern reptiles are cold-blooded—they rely on the heat of the Sun to warm them up, and this means that they cannot live in cold places. They also have less stamina than warm-blooded mammals and birds, which turn food energy into body heat. Dinosaurs and their relatives are classified as reptiles, so they were once seen as cold-blooded, scaly creatures a lot like modern lizards. But most experts now argue that all dinosaurs—and pterosaurs—were warm-blooded. This has revolutionized the way we see these animals, especially because many of the smaller ones, at least, are now known to have had insulating fur or feathers to retain body heat.

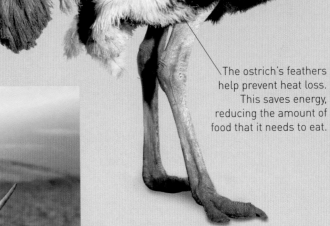

The ostrich's feathers help prevent heat loss. This saves energy, reducing the amount of food that it needs to eat.

Lizards and birds
Cold-blooded modern reptiles such as lizards sprawl on the ground, easily run out of energy, and cannot stay active in cold weather. By contrast, this warm-blooded ostrich has powerful legs that support its body, and it can run very fast for long distances without tiring. It can also stay active on the coldest nights.

Agile hunters
Small, agile dinosaurs do not look like lizards—they look like birds. Their skeletons show that their legs supported their bodies, just like those of an ostrich. Even this traditional, featherless portrayal of two lightweight hunters depicted them as athletic, fast-moving creatures—a way of life that is typical of warm-blooded animals. In the 1960s, scientists started to wonder if dinosaurs might be warm-blooded, too.

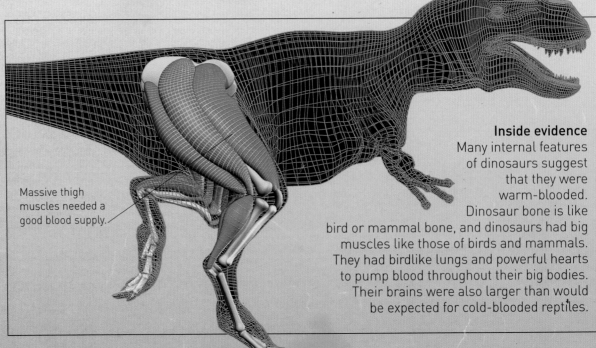

Massive thigh muscles needed a good blood supply.

Inside evidence
Many internal features of dinosaurs suggest that they were warm-blooded. Dinosaur bone is like bird or mammal bone, and dinosaurs had big muscles like those of birds and mammals. They had birdlike lungs and powerful hearts to pump blood throughout their big bodies. Their brains were also larger than would be expected for cold-blooded reptiles.

Growth rate

Dinosaurs grew surprisingly quickly. By analyzing fossils such as this thighbone of the giant sauropod *Apatosaurus*, scientists have shown that the animal could have reached full size within 10 or 12 years. This is strong evidence in favor of warm-blooded dinosaurs, because warm-blooded animals grow faster than cold-blooded ones. It also suggests that the agile, high-speed hunters and the gigantic plant eaters had the same basic biology.

Deep freeze

The Mesozoic climate was warmer than ours, but it had its cold regions. In the Cretaceous, the south coast of what is now Australia lay within the Antarctic Circle and would have had several months of total darkness and freezing temperatures. Despite this, the remains of dinosaurs have been found there. They must have been warm-blooded in order to survive such cold winter conditions.

The body of the theropod hunter *Sinornithosaurus* was insulated with soft, downy feathers.

Long feathers on its arms may have helped *Sinornithosaurus* brood its young, or they may have been for show.

Insulation

Roughly 80 percent of the food that a warm-blooded animal eats is turned into body heat. If it loses heat, it must eat more. So insulation is vital, especially for smaller animals that easily lose heat. Feathers provide excellent insulation, and traces of feathers have been found on many fossils of nonflying dinosaurs. Pterosaur fossils show traces of hair. This is powerful evidence that these animals were warm-blooded.

Plateosaurus

While one branch of the saurischian dinosaurs evolved into meat-eating theropods like *Coelophysis*, another gave rise to plant-eating sauropodomorphs such as *Plateosaurus*. This was one of the prosauropods, which were the main herbivores of the Late Triassic. Although bigger than most of them, *Plateosaurus* was a lot lighter than the colossal sauropods of the Jurassic, and unlike them, it probably walked on its hind legs. *Plateosaurus* seems to have been common in what is now Europe. Many skeletons have been found together, indicating that it lived in herds, migrating over the plains in search of food.

FAST FACTS

NAME MEANS: "broad lizard"
DATE: 216–203 mya

TRIASSIC | JURASSIC | CRETACEOUS
251 MYA | 199 | 145 | 65 MYA

LENGTH: 30 ft (10 m)

FOSSIL FINDS: Europe

DIET: Herbivore

Like other prosauropods, this animal ate mostly plants, reaching up to browse on cycads and conifers. Its small slicing teeth overlapped like scissor blades to shear through leaf stems and had rough surfaces for shredding the tough foliage.

With its long neck, *Plateosaurus* could get at leaves that were out of reach of other Triassic plant eaters. Its main competitors were other prosauropods, but most of these were smaller. Its high vantage point also gave it early warning of any approaching threats.

The skin seems to have been tough and scaly, like that of a large lizard. The scales protected the skin from scratches and helped prevent moisture loss. This was important in the Triassic, when the climate was hot and dry. It may have enabled *Plateosaurus* herds to make long treks through arid terrain.

Hands and feet

The prosauropods evolved from much smaller meat-eating dinosaurs, and the smallest ones probably resembled *Eoraptor*—an early two-footed hunter. During the Late Triassic and Early Jurassic, they evolved larger and larger forms, which may have spent more time on all fours. Despite this, they all had distinct hands with long fingers and thumbs rather than weight-supporting front feet like the later sauropods.

Favored sites

Plateosaurus is the best known of the prosauropods and one of the most common dinosaur fossils. Dozens of skeletons preserved in Triassic sandstones have been unearthed in more than 50 locations in Europe. Some of these sites may have been favored feeding or breeding areas, with herds of animals returning year after year. Alternatively, the bones could have been washed together by floodwater.

Although shorter than its hind limbs, its front limbs were long enough to allow *Plateosaurus* to lean on its hands to feed on low-growing plants. But recent research shows that it could not turn the palms of its hands downward, so it could not easily walk on them.

A long, heavy tail balanced the front end of the body, enabling the animal to walk on its hind legs and rear up to feed.

The hands could grasp branches when feeding.

Long, powerful legs supported the animal's weight and allowed it to reach high into the treetops. It could probably run on its hind legs, and despite its size and weight, *Plateosaurus* may have been able to move quite fast.

The powerful thumb claw might have been used for defense or fights between rival males.

These animals mostly propelled themselves with their tails but would have used the long flippers for turning and small maneuvers.

Bone bed
Shonisaurus is known mainly from a single site in Nevada. A mass of bones found in the 1920s turned out to be the skeletons of 37 of these giant animals, the biggest being 50 ft (15) m long. Much later, in the 1990s, the bones of a similar animal were discovered in British Columbia, Canada—but it was even bigger at 70 ft (21 m). This makes it the largest marine reptile ever found, although smaller than a blue whale.

Shonisaurus

The ichthyosaurs were a group of dolphinlike marine reptiles that flourished in the world's oceans throughout most of the Mesozoic era, but disappeared some 90 million years ago. This was one of the biggest—a whale-size beast that lived in the Late Triassic. It probably hunted fish, as well as squids and similar creatures such as ammonites. Like all ichthyosaurs, *Shonisaurus* would have spent its entire life at sea, although like any reptile, it had to breathe air.

Big *Shonisaurus* skulls do not have any teeth, and smaller ones have them only at the front of their jaws. It seems that the animal did not need teeth and lost them with age.

Lazy giant
Although one of the biggest ichthyosaurs, *Shonisaurus* was relatively primitive. Later ones, such as *Ichthyosaurus* itself, were more dolphinlike, with bigger tail fins. They could swim much faster to catch prey and escape danger.

The tail was formed from a fleshy fin above a downturned extension of the backbone. It was a lot like the tail of a typical shark, but the other way around—and since the fin was quite small, it would almost certainly have been much less useful for propulsion.

The long, narrow snout was shaped like the bill of a large bird. It could be easily swung from side to side to snatch passing prey, because it did not offer much resistance to the water.

As with other ichthyosaurs, the eyes were set in large sockets, each enclosed by a bony ring. This may have protected the eye from damage when hunting or helped resist intense water pressure during deep diving.

The flippers were much longer and narrower than those of most ichthyosaurs. Each had a complex skeleton made up of many small bones.

FAST FACTS

FOSSIL FINDS: North America

DIET: Fish eater

NAME MEANS: "lizard of the Shoshone Mountains"
DATE: 216–203 mya

	TRIASSIC	JURASSIC	CRETACEOUS	
251 MYA		199	145	65 MYA

LENGTH: 70 ft (21 m)

Three of the four fingers form a grasping "hand" at the front of the wing. The fourth finger is greatly elongated into a jointed strut that extends to the wingtip to support the leathery wing membrane.

FAST FACTS

FOSSIL FINDS: Italy

NAME MEANS:
"true two-formed tooth"
DATE: 216–203 mya

TRIASSIC	JURASSIC	CRETACEOUS
251 MYA	199	145	65 MYA

DIET: Fish eater

WINGSPAN: Up to 3 ft (1 m)

As with all pterosaurs, the wings were stretchy sheets of skin that were joined to the animal's thighs. They were reinforced with layers of strong, springy fibers embedded in the wing membrane, and these may have been linked to muscles that could adjust the wing profile.

Eudimorphodon

Long before birds evolved, there were other vertebrate animals hunting in the Mesozoic skies. They were pterosaurs—close relatives of dinosaurs—which appeared in the Late Triassic. *Eudimorphodon* was one of the earliest, a crow-size flying reptile with a long tail and a large head bristling with sharp teeth. These were of two main types, which explains its odd name. They indicate that it was a fish eater, and fish remains have been found among its fossils. It probably hunted along lake and seashores and over coastal lagoons.

Elusive ancestors
Pterosaurs seem to have appeared almost fully formed in the Triassic. Early ones like *Eudimorphodon* were clearly able to fly well, so they must have had flying ancestors, but the fossil evidence for this is proving very difficult to find. This is probably because these animals had slim, delicate bones that did not survive long enough to become fossils.

Pterosaur teeth
Compared to most dinosaurs, the Triassic pterosaurs had unusually complex teeth, with each animal having teeth of different shapes for specific jobs. Some later pterosaurs had teeth specialized for filtering food from the water or crushing shellfish, while others had no teeth at all.

The body of *Eudimorphodon* was covered by a dense coat of furlike fibers. These would have helped insulate it and stop it from losing body heat. They show that *Eudimorphodon* was warm-blooded, as you would expect for a large flying animal that needed a lot of stamina to stay airborne.

Like other Triassic pterosaurs, *Eudimorphodon* had a long tail. This probably had a small diamond-shaped vane on the end that would have helped it make tight turns in the air. Later pterosaurs had much shorter tails, with no vane.

Strong hind legs with stout claws would have enabled the animal to forage for food on the ground. It probably walked on both its back and front limbs, folding its wings up out of the way.

Eudimorphodon had long, fanglike teeth at the front of its mouth, ideal for seizing slippery fish. It had smaller, multipointed teeth at the back of its mouth, which it would have used to cut its prey into smaller chunks that were easy to swallow.

Compared to later sauropods, *Isanosaurus* had a short neck. But it could probably rear up on its hind legs to feed, and this helped it reach high into the treetops.

Like all animals that eat a lot of leaves, *Isanosaurus* needed a bulky digestive system. Big bones in its pelvis—found in all sauropods—meant that this was carried well forward of the animal's hind legs, so it had good reason to support some of its weight on its front feet when walking.

Long vertical extensions of the vertebrae—the bones of the spine—were linked by muscles and tendons that supported the back and tail.

The front legs were long, but not as long or massive as the hind legs. The front feet also had more mobile toes that may have been useful when feeding high in the trees.

Each hind foot was supported by a big wedge-shaped pad of fatty tissue, a lot like the foot of an elephant. This spread the load, leaving a broad oval footprint.

Sauropod herds

These big herbivores almost certainly lived in herds, a lot like wild bison and elephants do today. We know about this from the evidence of track ways—long lines of fossil footprints left in mud that eventually turned to rock. The animals would have roamed the landscape to find places where there was plenty of food. Many later herbivores seem to have made seasonal migrations between different feeding and breeding areas.

Isanosaurus

The Late Triassic saw the evolution of new types of plant-eating sauropodomorphs. Instead of walking on their hind legs like prosauropods, these creatures walked on all fours. This helped support their bodies and enabled some of their descendants to grow into the biggest, heaviest land animals of all time. They were the sauropods. One of the earliest was *Isanosaurus*, which lived in what is now Southeast Asia. It was a lot smaller than later giants, but it probably had the same way of life.

Although its skull has not been found, *Isanosaurus* probably had a small head with short jaws and leaf-shaped or spoonlike teeth for cropping leaves.

Despite its weight, *Isanosaurus* walked on its toes.

Skeletal evidence
The fossils of *Isanosaurus* are among the earliest known of any sauropod. Only a few bones have survived, but the tall-spined vertebrae are not like those of earlier prosauropods, and its thighbones are straighter and more like those of later giants. So scientists are confident that it is one of the first true sauropods.

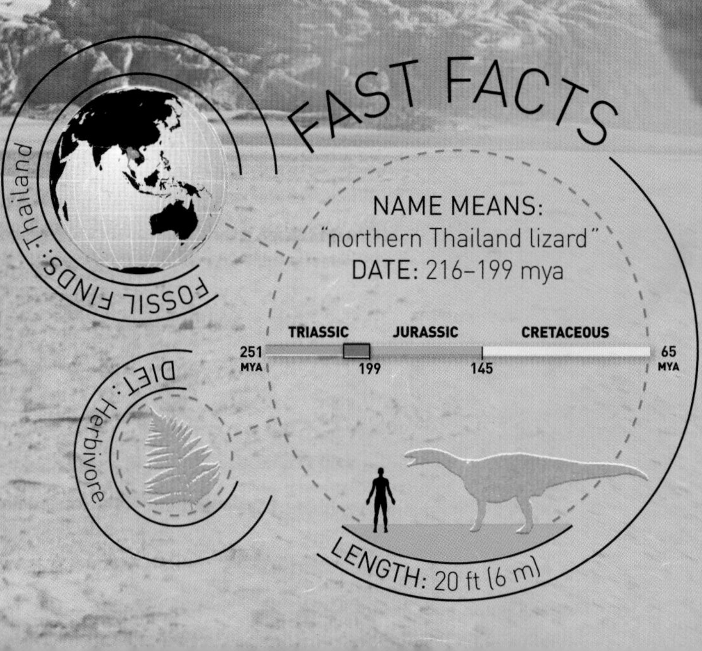

FAST FACTS

FOSSIL FINDS: Thailand

DIET: Herbivore

NAME MEANS:
"northern Thailand lizard"
DATE: 216–199 mya

TRIASSIC	JURASSIC	CRETACEOUS
251 MYA	199	145	65 MYA

LENGTH: 20 ft (6 m)

Jurassic world

The Jurassic was the second period of the Mesozoic era, which lasted from 199 to 145 million years ago. During this period, the vast supercontinent of Pangaea split in two, changing the climate and allowing lush vegetation and animal life to colonize much more of the land. This enabled dinosaurs and pterosaurs to flourish over a larger area. Dinosaurs evolved into a spectacular variety of forms, becoming the dominant large land animals. This was the period that saw the evolution of the huge plant-eating sauropods and the first truly big meat-eating theropods. A branch of the theropod line also gave rise to birds, which are still with us. Meanwhile, marine reptiles evolved as fearsome predators that dominated life in the oceans.

Continents and seas

As the Tethys Ocean grew wider, it split Pangaea into two main blocks—Laurasia and Gondwanaland. Meanwhile, the Panthalassic Ocean shrank to form the Pacific. Rising sea levels flooded continental margins with shallow seas, dividing large landmasses into smaller ones. As animals were isolated from one another by the water, they evolved in different ways.

Most of what is now the United States and Europe was underwater.

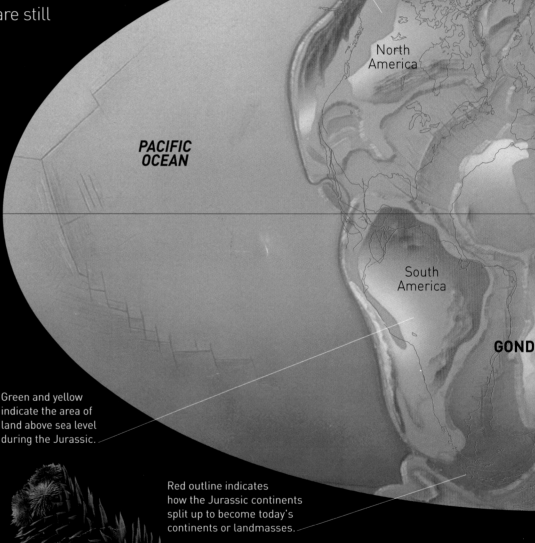

Alaska

LAUR

North America

PACIFIC OCEAN

South America

GOND

Green and yellow indicate the area of land above sea level during the Jurassic.

Red outline indicates how the Jurassic continents split up to become today's continents or landmasses.

Climate

The arid heart of the giant Pangaean landmass was eliminated as the supercontinent was split by the expanding Tethys Ocean. This made the climate much wetter and milder than in the Triassic and allowed forests to grow in regions that had once been dry and barren.

Plant life

During the Jurassic, plant life was more lush and widespread than in the Triassic. But the plants were similar, consisting of horsetails, ferns, club mosses, ginkgos, cycads, and conifer trees like this monkey-puzzle. There were still no flowering plants of any type, and certainly no grasses.

Dinosaurs

At the end of the Triassic, a lot of the dinosaurs' competitors became extinct. This gave dinosaurs the chance to take over by evolving new forms that were suited to different ways of life. This process eventually gave rise to giant plant-eating sauropods, more powerful theropod hunters, plated stegosaurs like this *Huayangosaurus*, heavily armored ankylosaurs, and the earliest ornithopods.

Siberia

ASIA

Europe

North China

The largest land area was eastern Laurasia—what is now Siberia, China, and Tibet.

South China

Turkey   Iran   Tibet

Indochina

Africa

TETHYS OCEAN

Arabia

Land invertebrates

Insects of many types flourished in the Jurassic forests, but since there were no flowering plants, there were no nectar-feeding insects such as butterflies and bees. There were definitely dragonflies, cockroaches, beetles, and flies, which were either hunters or fed on plants and dead material. There were also many other invertebrates such as spiders and scorpions that preyed on the insects, and myriapods resembling this modern pill millipede.

WANALAND

India

Australia

Antarctica

Australia and Antarctica were both part of the same landmass.

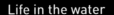

Protosuchus

Life in the water

The shallow seas that formed on the continental margins teemed with life, particularly ammonites and belemnites, which were relatives of modern squids. These were hunted by a variety of fish, and both were eaten by marine reptiles such as this *Ichthyosaurus*. In turn, the smaller ichthyosaurs were preyed upon by giant plesiosaurs.

Triassic survivors

The extinction event at the end of the Triassic eliminated almost all of the big land animals except dinosaurs and crocodylomorphs such as *Protosuchus*. The other main group of large Jurassic land animals were the pterosaurs. Early mammals were around but were quite small.

Big eyes on the sides of its head gave *Lesothosaurus* an excellent all-around view of any approaching threats. Such wariness is typical of small plant eaters.

Behind a beak were simple pointed teeth. These seem adapted for slicing through leaves and stems rather than grinding them to a pulp. This made the leaves less easy to digest, so *Lesothosaurus* may have eaten insects or carrion, too.

Powerful hind legs would have given *Lesothosaurus* a good turn of speed to escape its enemies, like a modern gazelle. It had four toes, but only three touched the ground.

The animal's front limbs were a lot shorter than its back ones, so they were not used for walking. Instead, they had long, grasping fingers.

Lesothosaurus

The first ornithischian dinosaurs were small animals that walked on two legs, so although they were plant eaters, they looked a little like the carnivorous theropods. *Lesothosaurus* is one of the earliest known, with simple teeth that were poorly adapted for pulping leaves, unlike those of many later ornithischians. Yet it was probably fast and agile, giving it a good chance of escaping hunters like this *Sphenosuchus*.

Primitive feature

The teeth of most ornithischian dinosaurs were inset from the sides of their jaws. This indicates that they had cheeks like ours, which stopped food from falling out of the sides of their mouths when chewing. *Lesothosaurus* does not have this feature, showing that it was a very primitive type of ornithischian.

Beak bone
All ornithischian dinosaurs had a special toothless bone at the tip of the lower jaw that helped support a beak. *Lesothosaurus* was one of the earliest dinosaurs with this adaptation, which may have made it more efficient at gathering plant food.

FAST FACTS

FOSSIL FINDS: South Africa

DIET: Herbivore

NAME MEANS:
"lizard from Lesotho"
DATE: 199–189 mya

TRIASSIC	JURASSIC	CRETACEOUS
251 MYA	199	145	65 MYA

LENGTH: 3 ft (1 m)

Like any animal that eats a lot of leaves, *Lesothosaurus* needed a big, heavy digestive system. But this was carried far back in its body, owing to the shape of its ornithischian pelvis. This meant that its weight was balanced over its hips, allowing it to walk and run on its hind legs.

Rhomaleosaurus

The Early Jurassic oceans were dominated by two main types of marine reptiles—dolphinlike ichthyosaurs and long-necked plesiosaurs. *Rhomaleosaurus* was a type of plesiosaur known as a pliosaur, with a shorter neck and a massive skull with powerful jaws. This made it a formidable oceanic hunter that preyed on other marine reptiles as well as large fish. It had a highly developed sense of smell for picking up the scent of prey at a distance and excellent eyesight for targeting its victims at close range. In many ways it was the Jurassic marine equivalent of *Tyrannosaurus rex*.

Like all plesiosaurs, this animal had a relatively short tail that may have had a low tail fin. Its sleek body was probably padded with fat beneath the skin to improve its streamlining, allowing it to swim faster.

The long, pointed interlocking teeth would have been ideal for seizing its prey. They were not, however, adapted for chewing or slicing through flesh, so it is likely that *Rhomaleosaurus* swallowed most of its smaller victims whole.

Sniffing the water

All marine reptiles breathed air, just like crocodiles. But although *Rhomaleosaurus* had nostrils on top of its snout, it did not use them for breathing. As it swam along, water was channeled into openings in the roof of its mouth that led to a nasal area lined with sense organs. These detected any scents in the water before it flowed out through the nostrils. Most plesiosaurs and related marine reptiles used the same system.

Although *Rhomaleosaurus* almost certainly ate a lot of fish, it is likely that it also preyed on ichthyosaurs and even smaller plesiosaurs like this one. Several plesiosaur bones have been found with deep pliosaur bite marks on them.

Pliosaurs such as *Rhomaleosaurus* had relatively short but very strong necks. Typical plesiosaurs had much longer, more flexible necks, and the Late Cretaceous *Elasmosaurus* had an amazing 72 neck bones (vertebrae)— more than any other known animal.

Shock tactics

The massive skull and long, strong teeth of *Rhomaleosaurus* were well suited to attacking big animals. It probably used the shock tactic of rushing in to cripple its victims with a few enormous bites, a lot like a great white shark. But since its teeth were not slicing blades, it may have reduced large prey to manageable mouthfuls using the same technique as a big crocodile—seizing it and twisting around in the water to rip it apart.

Pliosaurs had four long flippers that were the same shape. They would have used these flippers to drive themselves through the water. They swam with an "underwater flying" technique, like modern sea lions.

FAST FACTS

FOSSIL FINDS: England and Germany

DIET: Carnivore

NAME MEANS:
"robust lizard"
DATE: 199–175 mya

TRIASSIC	JURASSIC	CRETACEOUS	
251 MYA	199	145	65 MYA

LENGTH: 15–21 ft (5–7 m)

Teeth and diet

The nature of an animal's diet is often obvious from the shape of its teeth. Horses have flattened teeth for grinding tough plants to a pulp, making them more digestible. Cats have long stabbing teeth for killing prey and no chewing teeth at all. Many lizards have a lot of leaf-shaped, all-purpose teeth, and fish-hunting crocodiles have batteries of sharp spikes. Dinosaur teeth are just as variable, and this helps scientists figure out what the animals might have eaten. But it is not always clear exactly how they used them.

Chewers and grinders

Ornithischian dinosaurs had chewing teeth to pulp their plant food and make it easier to digest. The cheek teeth of hadrosaurs were small, numerous, and tightly packed together to form grinding surfaces. The worn teeth were constantly replaced by new ones growing up from below. Some other ornithischians, such as ceratopsians, had shearing cheek teeth that sliced food instead of grinding it.

This hadrosaur had batteries of grinding cheek teeth, but a broad ducklike bill instead of front teeth.

Browsers

Giant sauropods such as this *Barosaurus* had big peglike teeth that were ideal for cropping leaves from trees, but not for chewing them. So these massive animals must have swallowed their leafy food without processing it. They had gizzards (specially adapted muscular stomachs) that crushed the leaves to some extent, but mostly they relied on fermentation in the digestive system.

Sauropod teeth often show signs of heavy wear.

The shallow jaws were equipped with quite small muscles.

Their enormously long necks enabled huge sauropods to reach high into trees to gather leaves.

Hunters

Meat is easy to digest without chewing, so the teeth of predatory theropods were specialized for killing and butchering their prey. Many hunters such as *Velociraptor* had long back-curved blades that were serrated like steak knives. Tyrannosaurs had stout spikes for inflicting deadly bites.

Velociraptor had saw-edged blades for slicing through tough hide and meat.

Stout, sharp claws gave *Velociraptor* a secure grip on its prey.

Fish eaters

Most fish are covered with a layer of slippery mucus that protects the skin from damage and infections. But it also makes them difficult to catch, so the first priority for any fish eater is to get a grip. Modern fish-eating crocodiles and sharks have sharp, pointed teeth that pierce the slimy skin. Many marine reptiles, some pterosaurs, and fish-eating dinosaurs such as this *Spinosaurus* had similar teeth. Often the longest teeth formed an interlocking trap at the very front of the jaws. However, some Mesozoic fish hunters seemed to manage without any teeth at all, just like modern fish-eating birds.

Protoceratops was a primitive ceratopsian—a smaller relative of the mighty *Triceratops*. It grew to around 7 ft (2 m) long and weighed as much as a large pig.

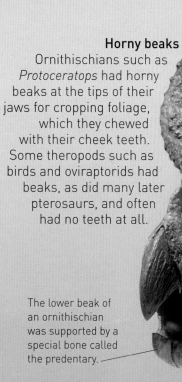

Horny beaks

Ornithischians such as *Protoceratops* had horny beaks at the tips of their jaws for cropping foliage, which they chewed with their cheek teeth. Some theropods such as birds and oviraptorids had beaks, as did many later pterosaurs, and often had no teeth at all.

Coprolites

Teeth are not the only evidence of diet. Fossilized stomach contents often contain seeds, fern spores, and bones—even entire skeletons. There are also fossilized dinosaur droppings, like these. Known as coprolites, they contain seeds, shredded stems, bone fragments, and even—in Late Cretaceous coprolites—the first evidence of grass.

The lower beak of an ornithischian was supported by a special bone called the predentary.

Heterodontosaurus

This small Early Jurassic dinosaur looks like a typical plant-eating ornithischian, except for one thing—its teeth. Most dinosaurs had teeth that were all very similar, but *Heterodontosaurus* had closely packed chewing teeth at the back of its mouth and long, pointed teeth at the front. The pointed teeth are like the canines of modern carnivores such as dogs, suggesting that it may have used them for eating meat. Yet other ornithischians ate plants, so this seems unlikely. Their true function is still a mystery.

The jaws were tipped with a horny beak, like those of other ornithischians. The beak was almost certainly used for gathering leaves.

Key discovery
The first fossil of *Heterodontosaurus* was discovered in South Africa in 1962. It was a single skull and jaw, but with most of its extraordinary teeth in place. A complete skeleton unearthed 14 years later is one of the finest ever found, with every bone intact.

The long, tapering tail acted as a counterbalance.

Heterodontosaurus had sturdy front limbs with strong, grasping hands, each with five clawed fingers. It may have used these to seize small animals as part of its diet.

A Jurassic pig?
Although the long, pointed teeth of *Heterodontosaurus* make it look like a fierce hunter, it probably fed mostly on plants. It was well equipped for chewing, which the predatory theropods were not, and it may have used its long teeth to dig up juicy roots or for defense. But it could have eaten small animals, too. Many modern mammals, such as wild pigs, have mixed diets, and maybe this was their Jurassic equivalent.

FOSSIL FINDS: South Africa

DIET: Mostly a herbivore

FAST FACTS

NAME MEANS:
"different-toothed lizard"
DATE: 199–189 mya

TRIASSIC	JURASSIC	CRETACEOUS

251 MYA — 199 — 145 — 65 MYA

LENGTH: 3 ft (1 m)

We do not know what the skin of this dinosaur was like, but it was probably scaly. Camouflage colors and patterns would have helped it hide from predators.

Roughly the size of a turkey, this animal stood on two legs. Being light and agile, it could probably run quite fast to get away from its enemies.

Big eyes on the sides of its head would have given *Heterodontosaurus* excellent all-around vision to check for danger while feeding.

A deep notch in the upper jaw made space for the very long lower "canine" teeth. These were almost like tusks, and it is possible that they were used for fighting.

Cryolophosaurus

This big meat eater is distinctive because it had a peculiar bony crest on top of its tall, narrow skull. Instead of running along its forehead, as with a few other crested theropods, it ran across the animal's head, just above its eyes. The crest was probably brightly colored and almost certainly played a part in dominance displays between rivals like these. A stronger animal may have had a more impressive crest. Apart from this odd feature, *Cryolophosaurus* is also unusual because its fossils were found in Antarctica, in one of the few ice-free regions of the Transantarctic Mountains.

The teeth were curved serrated blades, like those of most hunters. It also had a deep, strong jaw.

Crested theropods
During the Early Jurassic, dinosaurs began to diversify into many new forms of plant eaters and hunters. *Cryolophosaurus* belonged to a theropod group called the dilophosaurids, which were all distinguished by crests on their heads. They flourished in the Early Jurassic but then died out. Their place was taken by more advanced stiff-tailed theropods known as the tetanurans.

Unlike the tetanuran theropods that became so successful during the Late Jurassic and Cretaceous, *Cryolophosaurus* had four fingers on each hand instead of three. It may have used its hands to help seize prey.

The bones of a large plant-eating dinosaur known as *Glacialisaurus* were found near the remains of *Cryolophosaurus*. This animal may have been its main prey. Other bones included those of pterosaurs and small mammals.

The crest was curled over like a tuft of hair, and before it was given an official name, the dinosaur was known as "Elvisaurus," after Elvis Presley!

Despite its large head and jaws, *Cryolophosaurus* had a relatively slender, lightweight build. It was probably a fast runner.

FAST FACTS

FOSSIL FINDS: Antarctica

DIET: Carnivore

NAME MEANS: "frozen crested lizard"
DATE: 189–183 mya

	TRIASSIC	JURASSIC	CRETACEOUS	
251 MYA		199	145	65 MYA

LENGTH: 20 ft (6 m)

Buried treasure

Antarctic dinosaur fossils may be quite common, because in Early Jurassic times the continent lay much farther north and had a temperate climate with cycad and conifer forests. However, most of the rocks that might bear fossils are now buried beneath thick ice sheets.

Scelidosaurus

The Early Jurassic saw the emergence of the first armored dinosaurs—the thyreophorans. Later, these evolved into the plated stegosaurs and tanklike ankylosaurs, but early ones like *Scelidosaurus* just had small bony plates embedded in their skin. These plates, or scutes, were covered with tough keratin—the material of which fingernails are made. They were not connected to one another, so they did not form a rigid shield, but they would have posed a problem for any enemy. However, they would also have weighed the animal down, giving it less chance of running away.

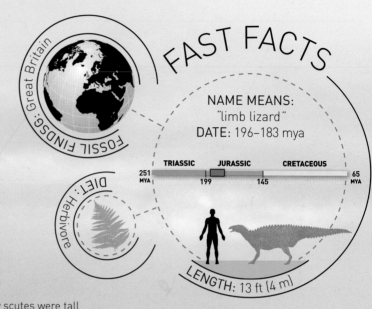

FAST FACTS

FOSSIL FINDSG: Great Britain

DIET: Herbivore

NAME MEANS:
"limb lizard"
DATE: 196–183 mya

TRIASSIC	JURASSIC	CRETACEOUS
251 MYA	199	145	65 MYA

LENGTH: 13 ft (4 m)

Defensive weapons
The main enemies of the plant-eating dinosaurs during the Early Jurassic were slender, fast theropods with bladelike teeth. If one of these attacked a *Scelidosaurus*, it would have broken its teeth on the bony scutes. But *Scelidosaurus* did not just rely on its armor for defense. It had a long tail that was also studded with bony plates. A single well-aimed blow with this would have crippled any attacker.

The bony scutes were tall knobs, almost like spikes. They formed several rows that extended down the animal's back—from its head to the tip of its tail. In between, the skin was covered with small, flat nonoverlapping scales.

It is more than likely that *Scelidosaurus* lived in herds that traveled together in search of good feeding grounds. Living like this would have been safer, especially for younger animals that would have been easier targets for hungry hunters.

The long front limbs indicate that *Scelidosaurus* walked on all fours, unlike earlier ornithischians. Its heavy armor would certainly have encouraged this. All the later thyreophorans have the same four-footed gait.

Acid solution

Scelidosaurus was one of the first dinosaur skeletons to be found in the world. It was unearthed in Great Britain in 1858. The fossil was buried in very hard limestone that was so difficult to remove that most of it stayed hidden for more than 100 years. But limestone can be dissolved by acid, and years of work using this technique have now revealed the entire skeleton.

The short, horny beak at the tip of the snout was backed up by small leaf-shaped or pointed teeth. The animal would have gathered food by browsing on low-growing plants.

Barosaurus

This dinosaur was one of the colossal plant-eating sauropods of the Jurassic. From head to tail, sauropods were the longest land animals that ever existed—especially *Barosaurus*, which had a particularly long neck. This enabled it to gather leaves from high in the tree canopy. What's more, its powerful hips, short body, and short forelimbs suggest that it often reared up on its hind legs to reach even higher.

The immense length of *Barosaurus* enabled it to reach up to at least 49 ft (15 m) and browse in treetops that were beyond the reach of other ground-based herbivores.

FOSSIL FINDS: North America

DIET: Herbivore

NAME MEANS: "heavy lizard"
DATE: 155–145 mya

TRIASSIC	JURASSIC	CRETACEOUS
251 MYA	199	145	65 MYA

LENGTH: 88 ft (27 m)

The very long whiplash tail might have made an effective defensive weapon against predators such as *Allosaurus*, which lived in the same habitat.

Food processor
These animals could not chew their food to make it easier to digest. Scientists used to think that they swallowed stones to help grind up the food in their gizzards (muscular stomachs), but there is no clear evidence of this. It is more likely that they gulped down vast amounts of leafy food and relied on bacteria living in their digestive systems to process it by fermentation. Some modern leaf-eating animals, such as the koala, use a similar system.

A row of spines extending all the way down the animal's back may have been a decorative crest or a defense feature. These spines were not part of the skeleton but were bony plates embedded in the skin.

Like all the diplodocids—named after *Diplodocus*, the most well known—*Barosaurus* had a very small head for its size. Its skull was relatively long and narrow, with a small cranium but a broad snout.

The skin was scaly. This provided protection from scratches and helped reduce moisture loss. If the animal was warm-blooded, it would not have needed much insulation because its bulk would retain body heat.

The eyes were set well back in its head, giving a good all-around view, especially when feeding high in the trees.

All the teeth were at the front of the jaw. The animal may have used them like a rake to rip leaves off twigs.

The massive pillarlike hind legs were like those of elephants, with the heels supported by wedges of fatty, fibrous tissue. Each forefoot had a single large claw.

Plates and spines

During the Jurassic period, some plant-eating dinosaurs developed a form of armor as protection against big killer theropods. Over time the armor became more elaborate, and while it remained partly defensive, it also became important for display and ritual combat between rivals, like the antlers of modern deer. The result was a wonderful variety of flamboyant plates, spines, and frills.

Many of the scutes studding *Gastonia*'s back and tail were extended into bladelike plates.

Dorsal plates

Most of the armored dinosaurs belonged to a group of ornithischians called the thyreophorans. They included the stegosaurs—spectacular animals with rows of plates and spines along their backs. *Kentrosaurus* was one of several that also had long spikes on its shoulders.

It is most likely that the immensely long shoulder spikes sported by *Kentrosaurus* had a defensive function.

The flat dorsal plates were almost certainly there to impress rivals rather than to deter enemies.

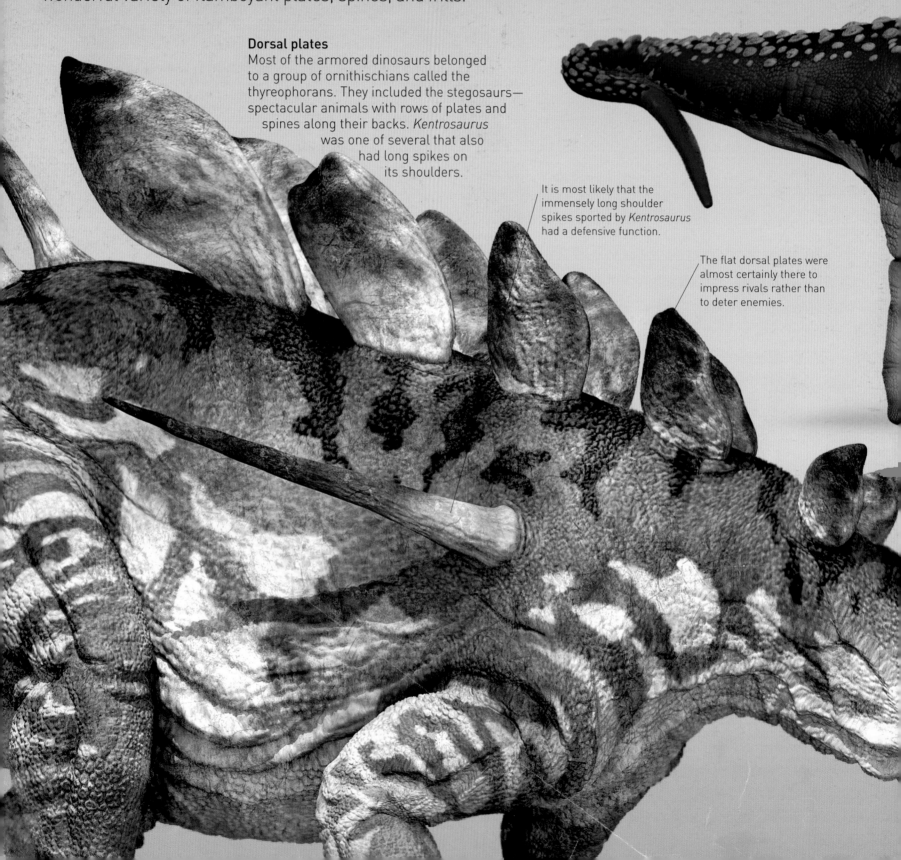

Heavy armor
Closely allied to the plated stegosaurs and part of the same thyreophoran group, ankylosaurs such as *Gastonia* were low-slung heavyweights with thick bony scutes on their backs. Their armor was clearly for protection, and some ankylosaurs had massive bony clubs on the tips of their tails.

Six big spikes and many smaller knobs adorned the neck frill, which may have been vividly colored.

The flat bony plates dotting the skin of *Saltasaurus* were for defense, not show.

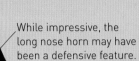

While impressive, the long nose horn may have been a defensive feature.

Frills and horns
In the Cretaceous, one ornithischian group developed bony neck frills that may have anchored extra-powerful jaw muscles. They evolved into extravagantly frilled and horned ceratopsians such as *Styracosaurus*, with its extraordinary array of spiked ornaments.

Defensive studs
Most armored dinosaurs were ornithischians, but many of the Cretaceous sauropods known as titanosaurs had bony studs embedded in their skin. These would have given them some defense against the huge predators of the time.

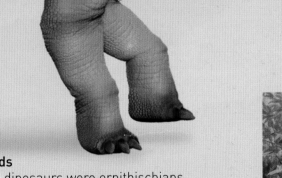

Devil's crown
Several of the Late Cretaceous pachycephalosaurs, or "bone heads," had various knobs and spikes crowning their thickened skulls. One of the most spectacular was *Stygimoloch*. Its name means "horned devil from the river of death"—a reference to the Hell Creek fossil site in Montana where its was found. Its spiked crown may have been useful in defense, but it was probably used for threat displays against rivals.

Stegosaurus

This well-known dinosaur was the biggest of the stegosaurs, one of the two main groups of armored thyreophorans. The stegosaurs were among the most common dinosaurs of the Late Jurassic, and their bones have been found all over the world. Their most distinctive features were the bony plates that sprouted from their backs. *Stegosaurus* itself had huge flat plates, but others had smaller plates or even spikes, and many had long spikes on their shoulders. Similar spikes on their tails would have been used for defense, but scientists still puzzle over the function of the plates.

FAST FACTS

NAME MEANS: "roof lizard"

DATE: 155–145 mya

TRIASSIC	JURASSIC	CRETACEOUS
251 MYA	199	145	65 MYA

LENGTH: 30 ft (9 m)

FOSSIL FINDS: North America and Portugal

DIET: Herbivore

Puzzling plates

When *Stegosaurus* was first found in the 1870s by fossil hunter Othniel Marsh, he thought its plates lay flat on its back, like roof tiles. This explains its odd name. One hundred years later, some scientists suggested that the plates absorbed or lost heat, depending on how the animal stood, helping it regulate its temperature. Most scientists now think they were display features, like flamboyant bird plumage.

The plates were not part of the skeleton but were attached to the skin by pads of tough cartilage. They were probably sheathed with horny keratin. The plates of some stegosaurs were paired, but *Stegosaurus* plates formed an alternating double row.

The front limbs were a lot shorter than the back ones, so *Stegosaurus* walked with its hips much higher than its shoulders. The bones of its spine were also very tall, and this gave the animal a high, arched shape. The huge alternating plates on its back added to this effect and made it look much bigger than it actually was.

Four big spikes stuck out sideways from the tip of the tail. *Stegosaurus* would have used these to defend itself by making crippling sideswipes at any attacking theropod, such as *Allosaurus*.

Stegosaurus had a long head with a narrow snout, tipped with a toothless horny beak. It probably used this to crop low-growing plants, which it then sliced up—rather than chewed—with its many small, leaf-shaped teeth.

The neck was protected by flexible armor made of small bony plates embedded in its skin, a lot like medieval chain mail. This would have made it difficult for a predator to kill it by going for its throat.

Allosaurus

Big predatory theropods appeared in the Middle Jurassic with the advent of the carnosaurs—fearsome hunters with knife-edged teeth that were specialized for attacking the stegosaurs and huge plant-eating sauropods of the time. One of the best known is *Allosaurus*, a giant killer that loosely resembled *Tyrannosaurus* but lived 70 million years earlier.

Slashing teeth

Although it was clearly a top predator that hunted big animals, *Allosaurus* did not have very powerful jaw muscles. It is possible that it attacked by opening its jaws very wide and slashing at its prey with its knife-edged teeth. They would have acted like a saw blade, slicing through flesh and causing a huge loss of blood, and the victim would have soon collapsed.

The long, pointed teeth were flattened from side to side with sharp serrated edges, like curved dagger blades. Teeth like this are ideal for slicing through meat but are not particularly strong. So *Allosaurus* would have targeted the softer parts of its victims, avoiding their bones.

Like all its close relatives, *Allosaurus* had a pair of bony ridges running down its snout. These may have strengthened the skull. But it also had a short triangular horn in front of each eye, and these horns were almost certainly just for show.

The jaw and skull of *Allosaurus* were very deep and narrow, and it could gape its mouth wide open to take huge bites. Its skull had big openings in the sides that made it lighter, but they reduced its strength. The openings may have contained air sacs that were linked to its lungs, as in modern birds.

FAST FACTS

NAME MEANS: "different lizard"

DATE: 155–145 mya

TRIASSIC	JURASSIC	CRETACEOUS
251 MYA	199	145	65 MYA

LENGTH: 39 ft (12 m)

FOSSIL FINDS: North America and Portugal

DIET: Carnivore

Sticky trap

Allosaurus seems to have been one of the most common large predators of the Late Jurassic. Just one site in Utah yielded the bones of more than 40 of them. It was once an area of sticky mud that trapped prey animals, attracting hungry hunters who became trapped in their turn.

The animal stood on long, powerful hind limbs, like all theropods. These seem to have been built for speed as well as strength.

The strong forelimbs had three-fingered hands armed with powerful claws, each up to 6 in (15 cm) long. *Allosaurus* probably used them like meat hooks to cling to its prey. They would have been especially useful when attacking big sauropods.

Allosaurus had four toes, with a small one pointing back and three much bigger toes pointing forward. This toe arrangement helped spread its weight.

Detailed fossils

Although it was one of the larger Late Jurassic pterosaurs, *Pterodactylus* is mostly important because of the quality of its fossils. Many were found in the very fine-grained Solnhofen limestones of southern Germany, which have preserved every detail of the bones and even show its wing membranes. They have helped scientists figure out exactly how pterosaurs were built and how they flew.

The very long snout may have been covered with a sheath of horny keratin, like a bird's bill. The snout would have been ideal for extracting marine worms from their burrows.

While the extended fourth finger supported the outer wing, the other three fingers formed a hand with sharp curved claws. *Pterodactylus* would have used its hands for walking and possibly climbing, as well as seizing prey.

The long jaws bristled with sharp, pointed teeth, especially at the front. Teeth like these are ideal for gripping slippery, struggling fish, so it is likely that *Pterodactylus* was a fish hunter. But it would have also preyed on other marine animals such as worms and shellfish.

Pterodactylus

This is the best known of a new breed of pterosaurs that appeared during the Late Jurassic. They had longer necks and much shorter tails than earlier pterosaurs, and the bones that formed their wings were much longer. They are known as pterodactyloids after *Pterodactylus*, which was first discovered in the late 1700s. *Pterodactylus* was originally thought to be some sort of bat, but its wing structure is different because the bones of just one finger support its wing. This is the origin of its name, which means "wing finger."

One *Pterodactylus* fossil found in 1998 clearly shows a lightweight crest of soft skinlike tissue on the skull. This would have been a display feature, like the crests sported by many modern birds, suggesting that it was also brightly colored.

The wings were membranes of skin and muscle. They were supported by the bones of the fourth finger and by tough tendonlike protein fibers that radiated from the arm and wrist.

The pterosaur's body was covered in hair—or by fibers that looked like hair—and it had a mane of longer hair on the back of its neck. This would have helped retain body heat, indicating that it was warm-blooded.

FAST FACTS

FOSSIL FINDS: Great Britain, France, and Germany

DIET: Mostly a fish eater

NAME MEANS: "wing finger"
DATE: 155–145 mya

TRIASSIC	JURASSIC	CRETACEOUS
251 MYA	199	145

65 MYA

WINGSPAN: 24 in (60 cm)

Beach hunter

Pterodactylus was superbly adapted for flight. But its big feet and other features indicate that it was a wader that hunted on beaches and in shallow lagoons. Fossil pterosaur track ways found in the 1990s show that it supported its weight on both its webbed feet and the hands at the bend of each wing, with its outer wings folded neatly upward.

The legs were long and slim, each with four clawed toes. The best fossils have traces indicating that the feet were webbed, like those of a pelican.

Dinosaurs and birds

Most scientists now agree that birds are small dinosaurs. They evolved from the mostly meat-eating theropods and gradually developed a variety of adaptations for flight that make modern birds seem very different from their Mesozoic ancestors. Yet the first birds were not unlike many other dinosaurs of the time, and their skeletons are almost identical. So dinosaurs are not extinct: they are all around us.

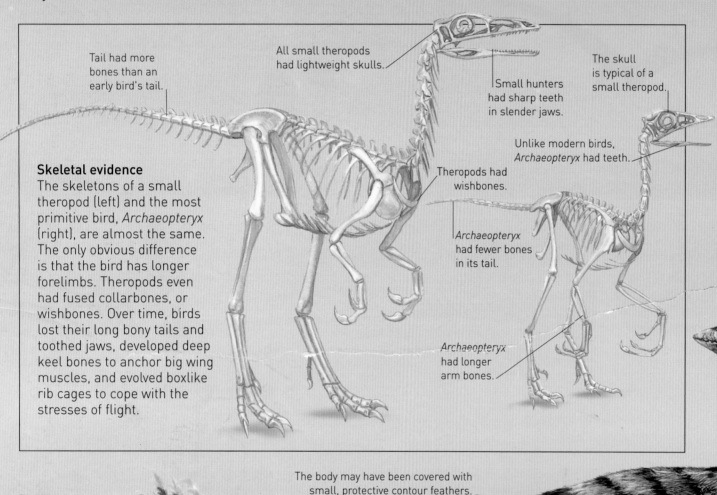

Tail had more bones than an early bird's tail.

All small theropods had lightweight skulls.

Small hunters had sharp teeth in slender jaws.

The skull is typical of a small theropod.

Unlike modern birds, *Archaeopteryx* had teeth.

Theropods had wishbones.

Archaeopteryx had fewer bones in its tail.

Archaeopteryx had longer arm bones.

Skeletal evidence

The skeletons of a small theropod (left) and the most primitive bird, *Archaeopteryx* (right), are almost the same. The only obvious difference is that the bird has longer forelimbs. Theropods even had fused collarbones, or wishbones. Over time, birds lost their long bony tails and toothed jaws, developed deep keel bones to anchor big wing muscles, and evolved boxlike rib cages to cope with the stresses of flight.

The long bony tail was adorned with feathery plumes.

The body may have been covered with small, protective contour feathers.

Beating its short "wings" may have helped propel the animal up trees.

Insulation and flight

Feathers began as insulation to conserve the energy of small warm-blooded dinosaurs. Fluffy "down feathers" are excellent for this. But other feathers are modified to form continuous vanes. They probably evolved for protection, but such vanes also have high air resistance. Many small theropods such as this *Protarchaeopteryx* had feathers like these, so in a sense they were all set up for flight.

The powerful legs were used for running rapidly over the ground.

Taking to the air

The first dinosaurs to take to the air probably glided from tree to tree like flying squirrels. They may have resembled *Microraptor*, a small, lightweight Early Cretaceous theropod that had feathers on both its front and hind limbs. You can clearly see them on this superb fossil. *Microraptor* could have swooped between branches without losing much height, but since it lacked big flight muscles, it was incapable of true powered flight.

Although males had long tail feathers, the bony tail was reduced to a short stump.

Despite its many advanced features, *Confuciusornis* had stout wing claws like the very first birds.

Energy supply

Powered flight requires plenty of energy, and this depends on a good oxygen supply. Modern birds have much more efficient lungs than we do, and the fossils of Mesozoic theropods show traces of the same type of lung anatomy. This was inherited by primitive birds like the Early Cretaceous *Jeholornis*.

Shedding weight

Theropods and primitive birds had several hollow, lightweight bones, and as birds evolved they acquired other weight-reducing adaptations such as slimmed-down skeletons, lightweight beaks, and much shorter bony tails. The Early Cretaceous *Confuciusornis* had all of these features, plus a shallow keel bone that would have provided anchorage for flight muscles.

Fully equipped

By the end of the Cretaceous, many birds such as the gull-size seabird *Ichthyornis* had evolved the deep keel bone and boxlike rib structure typical of modern birds. It was very different from primitive birds like *Archaeopteryx*—although it did have small, sharp teeth.

Archaeopteryx had many small, pointed teeth in the front half of its jaws, indicating that it fed on insects and possibly small lizards. The weight of the jaw and teeth would not have helped it get airborne.

Archaeopteryx

Dating from the Late Jurassic, *Archaeopteryx* was one of the first birds. It is certainly the earliest one found so far. Yet it was not like modern birds. *Archaeopteryx* had teeth instead of a beak and a long bony tail instead of a short feathered stump. More importantly, it did not have the deep keel bone that anchors the massive flight muscles of modern birds, so it would have been a weak flier at best. In fact, its skeleton was exactly like that of a small theropod dinosaur, except that its arms were extended to form long feathered wings.

Each foot had three forward-facing toes and a smaller toe at the back. The thighs were fully mobile from the hip, as in theropods, but unlike those of most modern birds, which are held close to the body.

Since it was a clumsy flier, *Archaeopteryx* was not an aerial hunter. But it might have swooped down on small animals running over the ground, like this lizard.

Scramble and glide

We can only guess how *Archaeopteryx* lived. Since its capacity for powered flight was limited, it is likely that *Archaeopteryx* spent most of its time on the ground, although the claws on each wing may have helped it scramble around in trees. It may have used its wings to glide between branches and back down to the ground.

Its powerful three-clawed hands were typical of a group of theropods called the maniraptorans, but its "arms" were unusually long—an adaptation for flying.

The flight muscles of *Archaeopteryx* must have been small, because it did not have an extra-deep breastbone to anchor them. Also, its skeleton was not strong enough to withstand the stresses of powerful wing beats. So it is likely that it was mostly a glider—able to hold its wings outspread, but little more.

The long tail had a central spine of bony vertebrae like the tail of a typical theropod but unlike that of a modern bird. The bones made it relatively heavy, but overlapping rows of feathers on each side would have made the animal more maneuverable in the air.

Fossil impressions of the large wing feathers show that they were broader on one side of the feather shaft, and the vanes were zipped together with tiny hooks. The flight feathers of modern birds are the same, showing that this animal had the right feathers for flight, even if it didn't have the muscle.

Feathered fossils

The first fossils of *Archaeopteryx* were found in 1861. They were discovered in fine-grained limestones that preserved every detail, including the impressions of feathers. Its odd features led scientists to view it as a "missing link" between reptiles and birds and as proof of Charles Darwin's recently published work on evolution. However, many years passed before scientists realized that it was a feathered theropod and what this might mean—that birds are actually living dinosaurs.

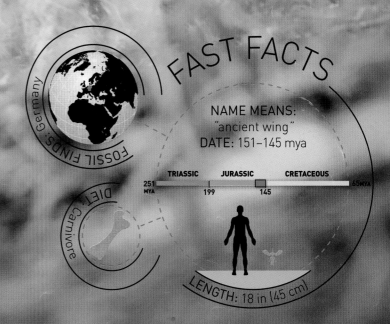

FOSSIL FINDS: Germany

FAST FACTS

NAME MEANS: "ancient wing"
DATE: 151–145 mya

	TRIASSIC	JURASSIC	CRETACEOUS	
251 MYA				65MYA
	199	145		

DIET: Carnivore

LENGTH: 18 in (45 cm)

Hunter and scavenger
The sharp, pointed teeth of *Compsognathus* indicate that it hunted small animals, and the first specimen ever found included the remains of a lizard in the stomach area of the fossil. Yet, like most hunters, *Compsognathus* would have almost certainly scavenged meat from the carcasses of animals killed by more powerful predators. It would have behaved like a jackal or crow, watching and waiting for any opportunity to snatch a free meal.

The slim, pointed, lightly built skull and jaw were typical of a creature that mostly preyed on small animals such as insects and lizards. Its pointed teeth were very sharp but did not have to be particularly strong.

Compsognathus

The word *dinosaur* conjures up images of colossal long-necked sauropods and predatory monsters like *Tyrannosaurus rex*. Yet many of the dinosaurs living at any one time were much smaller. *Compsognathus* is one of the smallest found so far—a slender, nimble theropod that was not much bigger than a chicken. It would have lived as many birds do now, chasing small prey and picking at scraps, such as the remains of dead animals.

Deadly relatives

This lightweight hunter is one of the advanced theropods known as the coelurosaurs, which appeared in the Jurassic at roughly the same time as powerful carnosaurs like *Allosaurus*. The coelurosaurs eventually gave rise to some of the most ferocious Mesozoic predators, including athletic dromeosaurs such as *Deinonychus* and *Velociraptor* and the massively built tyrannosaurs.

Compsognathus had a muscular yet lean, lightweight body, enabling it to accelerate rapidly and outrun small prey. Similar animals found in China were covered with fuzzy insulating protofeathers, and it is likely that *Compsognathus* had the same furry appearance.

Sharp eyesight would have been vital—both for catching a meal and keeping watch for danger. It might have been a hunter, but it was also prey.

Most of this animal's length is accounted for by its long tail, which provided balance when it was running fast.

Its long, yet slim legs enabled *Compsognathus* to run fast and pounce on fleeing prey. Its arms were relatively short but powerful, with big, strongly clawed thumbs for seizing its victims.

Like other theropods, it ran on the tips of three toes. A fourth backward-pointing toe was reduced to a stump.

FAST FACTS

FOSSIL FINDS: Germany and France

DIET: Carnivore

NAME MEANS: "pretty jaw"
DATE: 151–145 mya

TRIASSIC	JURASSIC	CRETACEOUS
251 MYA	199 — 145	65 MYA

LENGTH: 3 ft (1 m)

Cretaceous world

The close of the Jurassic, around 145 million years ago, is defined by a minor extinction event. This mostly affected marine life but may have had an impact on some types of dinosaurs such as the stegosaurs, which went into decline while other ornithischian groups prospered. The giant sauropods also became less dominant in the north but continued to flourish in other regions. Some of the plant eaters were armored to provide defense against meat-eating theropods. These included giants like *Tyrannosaurus*—a victim of the mass extinction that ended the Mesozoic era 65 million years ago. Meanwhile, mammals were becoming more diverse, and the world was transformed by the appearance of flowering plants.

Separating continents

The world became more recognizable as the Atlantic Ocean started to open up and South America and Africa became separate continents. But North America was split by a north-south seaway, and most of Europe was submerged by a shallow sea. India was a separate landmass, moving north toward Asia as the Tethys Ocean started to close up.

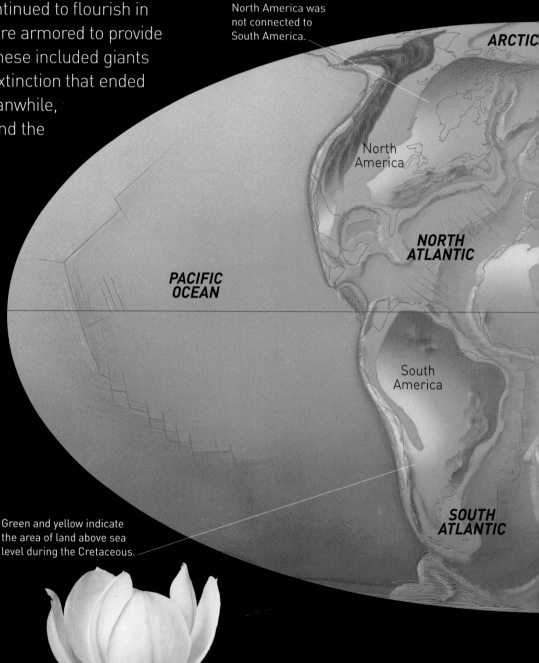

North America was not connected to South America.

ARCTIC

North America

NORTH ATLANTIC

PACIFIC OCEAN

South America

SOUTH ATLANTIC

Green and yellow indicate the area of land above sea level during the Cretaceous.

Climate

The warm, moist Jurassic climate continued in the Early Cretaceous, and the remains of Cretaceous palm trees have been found as far north as Alaska. But eventually, some parts of the world became more seasonal, with cold winters followed by warmer springs and summers.

Plant life

The greatest change on land was the appearance of flowering plants around 140 million years ago. Flowers like this magnolia attracted animals that carried their pollen, helping the plants reproduce. Conifers still flourished, but tree ferns, cycads, and ginkgos became less common. The first grasses also evolved in the Late Cretaceous.

Dinosaurs

The dinosaurs kept evolving new forms right up until the end of the Cretaceous. They included an amazing variety of different types, ranging from giants like this *Giganotosaurus*—a formidable hunter—to small feathered types that included many early birds. The pterosaurs declined, possibly because birds were so successful, but the remaining pterosaurs included the biggest flying animals that have ever existed.

Giganotosaurus was a giant theropod up to 39 ft (12 m) long.

OCEAN

Siberia

North China

Europe

South China

Indochina

Arabia

TETHYS OCEAN

Africa

India

Madagascar

Australia

Antarctica

Having opened in the Triassic, the Tethys started closing again.

Red outline indicates how the Cretaceous continents split up to become today's continents or landmasses.

Grasshopper

Land invertebrates

There was a marked increase in the variety of insect life in the Cretaceous. By the end of the period, most of the major modern insect groups had appeared, including termites, beetles, ants, wasps, bees, butterflies, and grasshoppers. Many of these insects fed on the nectar produced by flowering plants. As before—and ever since—they were hunted and trapped by a variety of spiders.

Life in the water

Fish of all types were common, along with marine invertebrates such as ammonites. Plesiosaurs hunted in the oceans throughout the period, but ichthyosaurs disappeared in the Late Cretaceous. Some birds took to hunting underwater like grebes, and some, such as this Late Cretaceous *Hesperornis*, were even flightless like penguins.

Mammals

During the Cretaceous, mammals were evolving into a variety of forms, including climbers, swimmers, and even gliders. Most were quite small, including this shrewlike *Eomaia*, but some were as big as badgers. Meanwhile, lizards and crocodilians flourished, and the first snakes appeared.

Sauropelta

This impressively spiked and plated creature was an ankylosaur—one of a group of bulky, heavily armored ornithischians that flourished until the very end of the Mesozoic era. Its armor was mostly defensive, for protection against fierce but quite lightly built predators such as *Deinonychus*. Yet its extravagance suggests that it had some social value, with bigger spikes giving an animal an advantage over its rivals.

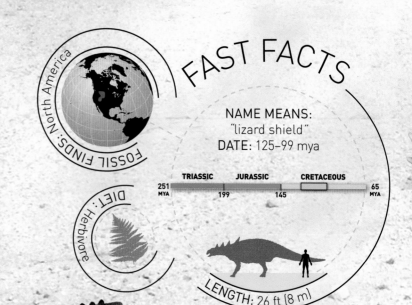

FOSSIL FINDS: North America

DIET: Herbivore

FAST FACTS

NAME MEANS:
"lizard shield"
DATE: 125–99 mya

	TRIASSIC	JURASSIC	CRETACEOUS	
251 MYA		199	145	65 MYA

LENGTH: 26 ft (8 m)

Rows of big, bony, tooth-breaking studs extended down the animal's back and tail, and the skin between the studs was reinforced with small bony nodules.

Heavy weapon
There were two main types of ankylosaurs. *Sauropelta* was one of a group called the nodosaurids, which had very spiny armor, particularly on their shoulders. The others—known as the ankylosaurids—were armed with very heavy clubs on the ends of their tails, which were stiffened to support the weight.

The long tail was fringed with bladelike plates that might have made very effective weapons when *Sauropelta* swept its tail from side to side. They could have done a predator a lot of damage.

The most imposing features of this animal were its immensely long neck spines. These had some protective value, but their dramatic appearance must have been just as important, making their weight worth carrying.

Effective deterrent
Although *Sauropelta* lived at the same time and place as *Deinonychus*, their remains have never been found together. By contrast, *Deinonychus* skeletons have been discovered near those of other herbivores. This may mean that the tooth-breaking armor did its job well, encouraging hunters to target less well-defended prey. Since later ankylosaurs evolved even heavier armor, it must have had some survival value.

Second thoughts
Some skeletons of *Sauropelta* have most of the armor intact, so we know how it fitted together. But the shoulder spikes were detached, and early reconstructions showed a single row of spikes on each side. Skeletal clues indicate that there were actually two rows, but we may never be sure unless a skeleton is found with the spikes in place.

Like all ankylosaurs, *Sauropelta* had relatively short, stocky legs and walked on all fours. Weighed down by its armor, it would have been a lumbering, low-feeding animal, a lot like a modern rhinoceros.

The broad, bulky body had plenty of room for a big digestive system. *Sauropelta* would have needed this to extract enough nutrients from its tough plant food.

Sauropelta had a beak at the tip of its snout for gathering low-growing foliage, which it mashed up with its many small leaf-shaped teeth. Its mouth was narrow, indicating that it was a selective feeder that chose the most nutritious leaves.

Deinonychus

This fast, agile hunter was one of the dromeosaurids, the most predatory of the advanced theropods known as maniraptorans, or "hand grabbers." It certainly had big, powerful hands with fearsome claws. More famously, each foot was equipped with a very large curved claw on the second toe that could be flipped up off the ground to keep it sharp. This sickle claw was almost certainly its main weapon, used for stabbing or ripping into its prey.

The teeth were typical of many meat eaters, being curved serrated blades that would have been very effective at slicing through skin and flesh, but not through bone. Powerful jaw muscles would have given the animal a fearsome bite.

The animal had big eyes that would have faced far forward to give it a degree of binocular vision—essential for an active hunter that needed to accurately target prey.

Like many theropods, *Deinonychus* had a slender, mobile, almost birdlike neck, giving its head a wide range of movement. Its body was probably covered with hairlike feathers for insulation.

FAST FACTS

NAME MEANS:
"false lizard"

DATE: 125–112 mya

TRIASSIC	JURASSIC	CRETACEOUS
251 MYA	199	145	65 MYA

LENGTH: 13 ft (4 m)

FOSSIL FINDS: North America

DIET: Carnivore

Breakthrough study
In the late 1960s, dinosaur expert John Ostrom made a study of *Deinonychus* that convinced him that it was a fast, agile, relatively intelligent predator and almost certainly warm-blooded. This triggered a debate about dinosaur physiology that has still not been resolved, although most scientists now agree with Ostrom. So *Deinonychus* all but destroyed the traditional image of dinosaurs as slow, stupid, cold-blooded reptiles.

The long tail may have had a fan of broad-vaned feathers at the end. It was held stiff and straight to balance the animal when it was on the move.

Pack hunter

On one fossil site several *Deinonychus* skeletons were found scattered around a single *Tenontosaurus* (see page 66). This suggests that *Deinonychus* hunted in packs, although it is not likely that it used such sophisticated tactics as modern wolves or lions.

The arms were long and strong, each with three big fingers equipped with stout, sharply curved claws. *Deinonychus* would have used these to cling to its prey when it launched an attack. Feathers on the forearms may have been useful when brooding eggs or young.

The enormous "killer claw" would have ripped into prey like a can opener, inflicting terrible wounds to weaken the victim.

Tenontosaurus

During the Cretaceous, North America was divided by a shallow sea that extended across the region that is now flat prairie. This big herbivore was one of the dinosaurs that roamed the coastal plains, feeding on the vegetation. It was a big ornithischian that unlike its smaller relatives, seems to have spent most of its time walking on four legs. It may have lived in herds, partly for protection from predators such as these marauding *Deinonychus*.

Success story
Tenontosaurus was a primitive iguanodont—one of a group of ornithopods that were the most successful of all the ornithischian dinosaurs. They flourished in the Cretaceous, especially in North America, where the giant sauropods became less common.

The jaws were tipped with a sharp horny beak for cropping leaves from low-growing plants, and it had no front teeth. Its cheek teeth were well adapted for shearing through vegetation to release the nutritious juices.

Its bulky body contained the big digestive system that *Tenontosaurus* needed to process large quantities of plant food. But its weight would have slowed the animal down, making it vulnerable to attack.

Tenontosaurus probably supported its weight on all four feet, since its front legs were relatively sturdy. But it might have been able to rear up to gather leaves from trees.

Soft target
As a big, relatively slow-moving plant eater, *Tenontosaurus* was a prime target for hunters. It did not have protective armor, and few weapons besides its clawed feet and long tail. Several *Deinonychus* skeletons were found with one specimen, and they were very likely to have been attacking it. On the other hand, the remains could indicate that it was able to fight back and kill its tormentors.

FAST FACTS

FOSSIL FINDS: North America

DIET: Herbivore

NAME MEANS:
"tendon lizard"
DATE: 125–112 mya

TRIASSIC	JURASSIC	CRETACEOUS	
251 MYA	199	145	65 MYA

LENGTH: 16–23 ft (5–7 m)

This animal had a very long tail with an unusually deep, thick base. It is possible that it was used as a defensive weapon.

A relatively small, lightweight hunter like *Deinonychus* had no chance of bringing down an adult *Tenontosaurus* if it was hunting alone. But a family group hunting together might have been more successful.

Spinosaurus

This spectacular predator was one of the biggest hunters of all time. It was longer than a tyrannosaur and probably heavier. Yet despite this, it seems to have been specialized for eating fish, because its fearsome teeth and jaws were just like those of modern fish-eating crocodiles. There were several similar species, all with the same crocodile jaws. Its size was enhanced by long bones extending up from its spine, which may have supported a tall dorsal crest, or "sail."

The weight of the long tail balanced the head and forelimbs, enabling *Spinosaurus* to walk on its hind legs. As with all the advanced theropods known as tetanurans, it had a stiff tail tip.

Sail or hump?

The mystery about *Spinosaurus* is the true purpose of its dorsal crest. Some scientists think that the bones supported a fatty, energy-storing hump, but the weight of this would have been a problem for an animal that stood on its hind legs. The tall bones were light, and it is more likely that they supported a flat "sail" that enhanced the animal's territorial displays. It may also have acted as a radiator, helping *Spinosaurus* lose heat in hot weather.

Long, powerful hind limbs supported the immense weight of the animal's body and allowed it to wade into deep water to hunt fish. It stood on the tips of three forward-facing toes, just like other theropods, and despite its size, it was probably agile.

The very powerful arms had three fingers with huge curved claws, ideal for hooking big fish out of the water.

The "sail" on the animal's back was supported by bones that, at their tallest, were up to 6 ft (1.8 m) long. They were extensions of the vertebrae, known as neural spines. All dinosaurs had these, but they were usually much shorter.

The remains of fish up to 10 ft (3 m) long have been found in rocks that contain spinosaur fossils.

The slender snout bristled with conical pointed teeth. The longest sprouted from the tip of the lower jaw and interlocked with the upper teeth, just like those of a crocodile. These long crocodile jaws were ideal for plunging into the water to seize fish.

FAST FACTS

FOSSIL FINDS: North Africa

NAME MEANS:
"spine lizard"
DATE: 125–99 mya

TRIASSIC	JURASSIC	CRETACEOUS	
251 MYA	199	145	65 MYA

DIET: Mostly a fish eater

LENGTH: 52 ft (16 m)

Prey

Spinosaurus was a very powerful predator, and there is evidence that it would have eaten other animals in addition to fish. The skeleton of a similar spinosaur called *Baryonyx* was found with the partly digested remains of a small dinosaur in its stomach.

Scales and feathers

For years, everyone thought that all dinosaurs had scaly skin, like typical reptiles. Some dinosaurs certainly did have scales, and some were armored. But recent fossil evidence shows that many small theropods were covered with feathers of some type. These would have helped them stay warm—indicating that they were warm-blooded. Bigger dinosaurs were so massive that their sheer bulk would have stopped them from losing vital body heat.

This fossilized skin fragment shows that *Triceratops* had rough, irregular scales.

Each scute had a bony base but was covered with keratin—the material that formed the animal's scales.

Protective scales

Some dinosaur fossils preserve impressions of their skin that show nonoverlapping bumpy scales, a lot like those of a tortoise. They would have protected the animal's skin and helped retain body moisture. This might have been important to dinosaurs that lived in dry climates.

The very long tail of this animal is typical of a small, fast-running hunter.

Bony scutes

Edmontonia was one of the armored ankylosaurs that had big bony plates embedded in their skin. Known as scutes, they gave some protection from predators. Other dinosaurs had similar but more ornamental plates.

Fuzzy feathers

Found in China in the 1990s, the fossils of small Early Cretaceous theropods such as *Sinosauropteryx* preserve traces of primitive fuzzy feathers. These protofeathers must have resembled those of a modern kiwi and almost certainly evolved as insulation.

The tuft of bristles on the tail of *Psittacosaurus* was probably for display.

This astonishingly well-preserved fossil shows most of the soft parts of the animal, as well as the strange brushlike spines on its tail.

Fluffy down feathers kept the animal warm on cold nights.

The dark line along the back is the remains of a fuzzy pelt of simple two-branched feathers.

Spiny plant eater

Some dinosaur fossils found in China show the remains of slender quilllike spines. The primitive ceratopsian *Psittacosaurus* had a tuft of quills on its tail, almost like a porcupine. Unlike other "fuzzy dinosaurs," this is an ornithischian. This suggests that these spiny, fuzzy, or feathery features were much more common among dinosaurs than we thought.

Feathered hunters

It is now clear that most small Cretaceous theropods were covered with feathers. Later ones such as this *Gallimimus* had branched feathers resembling the insulating down feathers of modern birds, and many also had stiff, broad-vaned plumes on their arms and tails.

Fine plumage

Feathers might have evolved as insulation, but they are also an opportunity for flamboyant display. They can be colored and iridescent, and since they are so light, they can be very long without weighing an animal down. The small Middle Jurassic theropod *Epidexipteryx*, shown here, is the earliest-known dinosaur with such ornamental feathers.

Citipati

Most dinosaurs were clearly hunters or plant eaters, but *Citipati* and its relatives are much less easy to pin down. Its skeletons, found in what is now the Gobi Desert in southern Mongolia, show that it was a theropod—a type of dinosaur that usually has the knifelike teeth of a carnivore. Yet *Citipati* had a short beak and no true teeth at all, although it did have two bony projections in the roof of its mouth. It belongs to a group called the oviraptorids, named after a similar creature called *Oviraptor*, or "egg-thief." They were once thought to eat dinosaur eggs, but there is no direct evidence of this.

Mixed diet?
One of the *Citipati* nests found in Mongolia contained the remains of two baby theropod dinosaurs, and it is likely that these were brought to the nest as food for the brooding adult. This suggests that these animals were at least partly carnivorous. But there is no reason why they could not have eaten eggs, too, as once suspected, and they might have eaten plants as well.

The stout beak was short, allowing the jaw muscles to exert a powerful closing force at the tip.

The two knobs that projected from the roof of the mouth would have been effective at cracking eggs, if this is what it ate.

The body was almost certainly covered with short filaments that looked like fur. These were actually simple feathers, but they still kept it warm.

A baby dinosaur would have been easy prey for this animal. It might have ripped it apart with its beak, just as eagles do today—and in fact, modern birds are close relatives of oviraptorids.

Oviraptorids such as *Citipati* were part of a theropod group called the maniraptorans, which had long arms with powerful hands and claws. Their forearms were fringed with long feathers like those of birds.

Good parent
Several fossils of *Citipati* have been found sitting on top of egg clutches, with their "wings" covering the eggs (see page 85). This brooding posture is found today only in birds. It shows that *Citipati* incubated its eggs and also that it had feathered forelimbs—since it would have needed these to protect the eggs.

A bony ridge on the skull would have supported a horny crest that formed part of the upper beak. Like the crest of a modern hornbill or cassowary, this was probably brightly colored. Extra plumelike feathers may have enhanced the visual effect.

FAST FACTS

FOSSIL FINDS: Mongolia

NAME MEANS:
"funeral pyre lord"
DATE: 83–70 mya

TRIASSIC	JURASSIC	CRETACEOUS
251 MYA	199	145	65 MYA

DIET: Mostly a carnivore

LENGTH: 10 ft (3 m)

Like all theropods, *Citipati* stood on powerful hind limbs with three functional toes. It was an agile, fast runner that would have resembled an ostrich or emu and could have been an effective predator.

Therizinosaurus

This spectacular animal is one of the strangest dinosaurs ever found. Its bones show that it was an early maniraptoran—a relative of the highly predatory *Deinonychus* and *Velociraptor*. Yet its teeth and digestive system were those of a herbivore, so it seems to have been a plant-eating theropod. Despite this, it was well able to protect itself, thanks to the astonishingly long, sharp claws on its hands, and even tyrannosaurids like this *Tarbosaurus* would have found it a dangerous target.

Instead of the bladelike teeth of a hunter, *Therizinosaurus* had small leaf-shaped teeth for chewing leaves. It even had a beak at its jaw tips, a lot like that of a plant-eating ornithischian.

Treetop browser
The fossils of *Therizinosaurus* and some of its relatives have been found in southern Mongolia, in part of what is now the cold, arid Gobi Desert. During the Late Cretaceous, this region was warmer and wetter, and there is evidence of tall trees. This fits in with the animal's anatomy, since its immense height was almost certainly an adaption for gathering leaves like a giraffe.

Therizinosaurus had a small, slender head and an elongated neck that allowed it to reach high up into the treetops to gather leaves and other plant food. There were other therizinosauroids, but this is the biggest found so far.

FAST FACTS

NAME MEANS:
"scythe lizard"
DATE: 83–70 mya

TRIASSIC   JURASSIC   CRETACEOUS

251 MYA   199   145   65 MYA

LENGTH: 26–36 ft [8–11 m]

FOSSIL FINDS: Mongolia and Kazakhstan

DIET: Herbivore

As a maniraptoran, *Therizinosaurus* had long arms that were probably adorned with colorful feathers. It may have used these to keep its young warm at night.

The most amazing features of this animal were its colossal claws. The longest claw bones measure 28 in [71 cm], and each would have been covered with a horny sheath up to half as long again. They would have been lethally effective weapons.

The body was much bulkier than that of a typical theropod. This is because it had to accommodate the big digestive system that it needed to process tough, high-fiber plant material. Despite this, it stood on its hind legs, just like any meat-eating theropod.

Tarbosaurus, a tyrannosaurid that lived at the same time in what is now central Asia, was *Therizinosaurus's* most dangerous enemy. Like *Tyrannosaurus* itself, *Tarbosaurus* was a massively powerful predator with huge jaws.

Plant-eating theropods

With their small heads, long necks, and big bellies, the therizinosauroids were some of the least typical theropods. Oddest of all is the way they seem to have been adapted to eat plant material instead of meat. In some ways, they resembled the modern giant panda, which is a very specialized type of bear and therefore technically a carnivore. However, the panda has evolved various physical adaptations that enable it to feed almost entirely on bamboo.

Crests and colors

Many fossils of dinosaurs and pterosaurs show traces of features that must have been at least partly for show. Odd bones on their heads, for example, probably supported more elaborate structures made of horn or were adorned with feathers. Some of these may have been useful for defense, but this does not explain why they were so spectacular. However, many modern animals have adaptations that enhance their territorial and courtship displays, and there is no reason why Mesozoic animals would have been any less flamboyant.

Crowned theropods
Powerful hunters rarely need to worry about defense, so the crests sported by some predatory theropods were almost certainly ornamental. *Guanlong*, an early tyrannosauroid discovered recently in China, had a crest on top of its snout. It was made of very thin bone to keep its weight to a minimum, and this indicates that it was mostly for show.

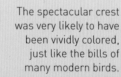

The lightly built crest on the head of *Guanlong* may have been crowned with a tuft of feathers to increase its visual impact.

Crested hadrosaurs
Many of the more dramatically crested dinosaurs were hadrosaurs, or duckbills—ornithopod vegetarians that probably lived in big groups. Hadrosaurs like this *Corythosaurus* would have used their colorful crests to add drama to displays aimed at rivals and potential mates. Males may have had more conspicuous crests, and in some cases such as *Parasaurolophus* (see page 78), chambers within the crest may have added resonance to their calls.

The spectacular crest was very likely to have been vividly colored, just like the bills of many modern birds.

Bizarre pterosaurs
Some pterosaurs had crests that almost defy belief. One of the most dramatic belonged to *Tupandactylus*, which lived in the Early Cretaceous in what is now Brazil. Supported by two bony struts, the flamboyant "sail" on its head was mostly made of horny tissue, a lot like the material that forms a bird's bill.

Big cavities in the frill would have reduced its value as armor, but made it lighter.

Elaborate frills

The horned and frilled ceratopsians look as if they used their headgear to keep predators at bay. This may have been partly true for some, such as *Triceratops* (see page 80). Yet the Late Cretaceous *Pentaceratops* had a much bigger neck frill than it would need for defense. It was probably for display, and animals with extra-large frills may have enjoyed high social status.

Fans and plumes

Fossils of the small maniraptoran theropod *Caudipteryx* show fanlike tail feathers, as well as plumes on its arms. It could not fly, so its tail fan was almost certainly for display and may have been brightly colored. Although it probably used its "wing feathers" for brooding eggs and young, they could have been just as colorful.

The head may have sported a crest of short feathers, but there is no evidence of anything more flamboyant.

Caudipteryx would probably have spread its tail feathers to give them more visual impact.

The feathers on the arms were both the wrong shape and too short for flight.

Blood flowing through the thin walls of inflatable air sacs would make them glow pink or red.

Red flush

One of the most complete dinosaurs ever found in Australia, *Muttaburrasaurus* had a hollow bony bump on its snout that may have supported a pair of inflatable air sacs. These could have functioned as sound chambers, making the animal's calls louder, and they might have flushed red like the comb of a rooster.

Muttaburrasaurus was a big plant-eating ornithopod that lived during the Early Cretaceous period.

Parasaurolophus

The hadrosaurs were the most advanced and successful of the plant-eating ornithopods, with very efficient chewing teeth for pulping their leafy food. They included the lambeosaurines, which had hollow bony crests on their heads. *Parasaurolophus* was one of the most spectacular of these, with a crest that, in some cases, doubled the length of its skull. The cavity inside was linked to its nostrils, and it may have used it to generate loud, penetrating calls.

FAST FACTS

NAME MEANS:
"near *Saurolophus*"

DATE: 83–65 mya

TRIASSIC	JURASSIC	CRETACEOUS
251 MYA	199	145	65 MYA

FOSSIL FINDS: North America

DIET: Herbivore

LENGTH: 33 ft (10 m)

Mobile teeth

All hadrosaurs had batteries of many small teeth that formed coarse grinding surfaces. According to one theory that is still disputed, the top jaw was pushed outward by pressure from the lower jaw as the animal chewed, so the upper teeth slid sideways against the lower ones. This would have maximized the grinding effect, making food easier to digest.

The animal gathered its leafy food with a broad ducklike beak, like all hadrosaurs—which are also known as duckbills. It was then mashed up by the highly effective chewing teeth in its cheeks.

The tall crest was supported by a long hollow bone extending back from the skull. Inside were a series of tubes with soft, moist linings, connected to the nostrils and possibly acting like a trumpet.

Social calls

If *Parasaurolophus* and its relatives were able to make trumpeting calls, they must have been highly social animals. It is also likely that they lived in dense forests, because sound is the best way of keeping in touch among thick vegetation. Despite this, they probably performed visual displays, too, enhanced by their imposing crests.

Parasaurolophus was one of the bulkiest of the lambeosaurines. Compared to its relatives, it had very chunky limbs and massive shoulder and hipbones. It also had tall neural spine bones extending upward from its backbone, and these increased the height of its back.

The pitch of the animal's call was affected by the length of its crest. A long crest would produce a lower note than a short one, so each species sounded different.

Like other hadrosaurs, this animal was able to walk on either two legs or four. It probably foraged for food on four legs but could run on two. However, it had a big body containing a large digestive system and so could not have been very agile.

Triceratops

One of the most well-known dinosaurs, *Triceratops* was the biggest of the ceratopsians—the frilled and horned herbivores that were so successful in the Late Cretaceous. Although less flamboyant than some, it made up for this with its sheer size. It was also one of the last of the Mesozoic giants, surviving until the great extinction that ended the era.

Rivers and plains

The remains of *Triceratops* have been found only in the eastern foothills of the Rocky Mountains in North America. In the Late Cretaceous, this region was a wooded plain, drained by rivers flowing into a sea covering the center of the continent.

FAST FACTS

FOSSIL FINDS: North America

DIET: Herbivore

NAME MEANS:
"three-horned face"
DATE: 70–65 mya

TRIASSIC	JURASSIC	CRETACEOUS	
251 MYA	199	145	65 MYA

LENGTH: 30 ft (9 m)

The size of an elephant, and with a massive neck shield of solid bone, this animal stood on all four feet and fed close to the ground. Its legs were strongly built to support its weight.

Defense or display?

Triceratops would have been at risk from the giant tyrannosaurs that lived at the same time, so it is likely that its horns and stout neck frill were partly defensive. The animals also seem to have lived in herds for mutual defense. Yet its headgear was very impressive, so it is just as likely that it was used to settle disputes within the herd, such as between rival males.

Many ceratopsians had large holes in the bones supporting their neck frills, but the frill of *Triceratops* was solid. It was bordered by small bony knobs but did not have many other ornaments.

Triceratops gets its name from the three long horns on its head—the two long brow horns extended to a magnificent 4 ft (1.2 m) or more.

The horny, toothless beak at the front of the animal's snout was ideal for gathering leaves, and its closely packed cheek teeth sheared against one another like scissors to slice up each mouthful. As with all dinosaurs, the teeth were replaced as they wore out.

Fossilized skin fragments show that *Triceratops* was covered with nonoverlapping scales that would have protected it from cuts and grazes.

The top of the skull was 8 in (20 cm) thick, which is at least 20 times thicker than the skull of a normal dinosaur of its size. This massively reinforced dome was surrounded by an impressive crown of strong spikes.

Like all other ornithischians, *Pachycephalosaurus* had a horny beak at the tip of its snout. It also had narrow jaws, a feature typical of animals that carefully choose their food. The jaws suggest that it avoided eating tough, indigestible vegetation.

So far the only known fossils of *Pachycephalosaurus* are skulls, and its body form has been based on the bones of relatives. Yet it was clearly a big animal, weighing up to 1,000 lb (450 kg).

Bone heads

The thickened skull of *Pachycephalosaurus* must have had an important function to make carrying its weight worthwhile. The animal might have used it to ram its enemies or rivals. Sparring males may even have fought by butting their heads together, as some wild sheep do today, but there is no damage to the skulls that might suggest this. It is possible that they just pushed against each other until the weaker animal gave in.

The long tail had a stiffened tip, making it easier for the animal to hold it out straight to balance the weight of its body. This indicates that *Pachycephalosaurus* was a fast, agile runner.

Pachycephalosaurs stood on their long, powerful hind legs and had relatively small front limbs. Each foot had three functional toes with stout claws and a shorter fourth toe at the back.

Pachycephalosaurus

One of the last major groups of dinosaurs to appear in the Mesozoic era were ornithischians with hugely reinforced skulls—the pachycephalosaurs, or "bone heads." They get their name from *Pachycephalosaurus*, the largest found so far. It had an amazingly thick cranium ringed with bony spikes and more spikes on its muzzle and cheeks. The function of all this heavyweight headgear is not clear, but it probably had more to do with rivalry than defense.

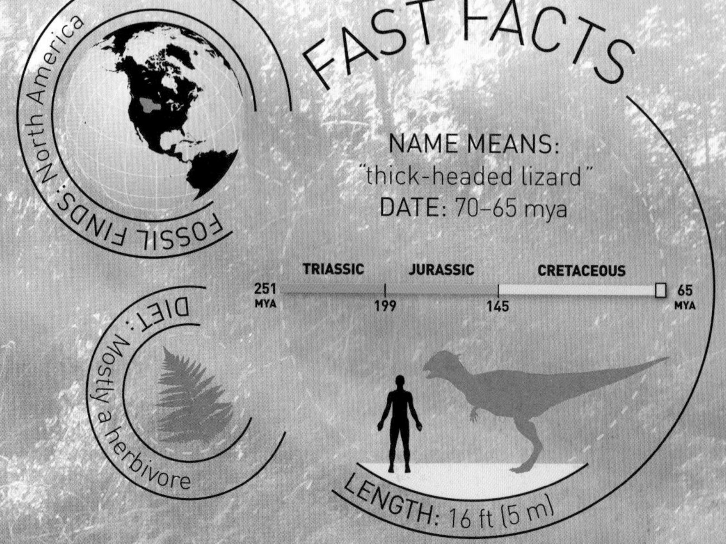

Broad diet

Like all its close relatives, *Pachycephalosaurus* had more than one type of tooth in its jaws. The small cheek teeth were leaf shaped, like those of many other plant-eating ornithischians, but it also had some conical teeth at the front of its jaws. They indicate that it ate a wide variety of plant foods and possibly a few small animals.

FOSSIL FINDS: North America

DIET: Mostly a herbivore

FAST FACTS

NAME MEANS: "thick-headed lizard"
DATE: 70–65 mya

TRIASSIC	JURASSIC	CRETACEOUS	
251 MYA	199	145	65 MYA

LENGTH: 16 ft (5 m)

The eyes faced far forward, so the animal must have had a degree of binocular vision. This would have helped it judge distances—possibly in connection with fighting.

Eggs and young

Although Mesozoic marine reptiles gave birth to live young, all dinosaurs and pterosaurs laid eggs. Some seemed to leave the eggs to develop untended, like many modern reptiles. But others definitely looked after them just as birds do—incubating the eggs in a nest and brooding the young with their body heat. Some dinosaurs formed breeding colonies, and there is evidence that they fed and defended their young for several months.

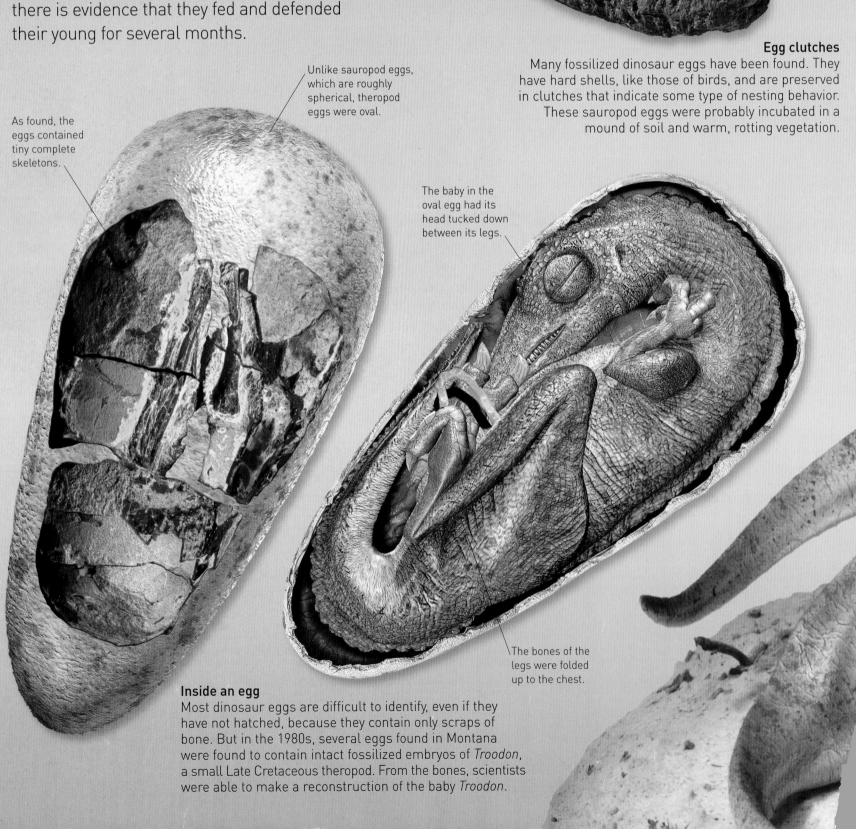

Egg clutches
Many fossilized dinosaur eggs have been found. They have hard shells, like those of birds, and are preserved in clutches that indicate some type of nesting behavior. These sauropod eggs were probably incubated in a mound of soil and warm, rotting vegetation.

Unlike sauropod eggs, which are roughly spherical, theropod eggs were oval.

As found, the eggs contained tiny complete skeletons.

The baby in the oval egg had its head tucked down between its legs.

The bones of the legs were folded up to the chest.

Inside an egg
Most dinosaur eggs are difficult to identify, even if they have not hatched, because they contain only scraps of bone. But in the 1980s, several eggs found in Montana were found to contain intact fossilized embryos of *Troodon*, a small Late Cretaceous theropod. From the bones, scientists were able to make a reconstruction of the baby *Troodon*.

Incubation

In the early 1990s, a site in the Gobi Desert yielded a skeleton of *Citipati* (see page 72) in the act of incubating a nest of 22 eggs. Its long, almost certainly feathered arms were spread over the eggs to keep them warm, as you can see from this fossil. Related animals such as *Deinonychus* (see page 64) have also been found in close contact with eggs. So it seems that many smaller, lighter feathered dinosaurs incubated their eggs like birds.

Nesting colonies

Some dinosaurs nested together in groups. In the 1970s, the remains of a whole colony were found in Montana. The nests were closely packed together, as in modern sea bird colonies. Each nest was a mound of soil, with a hollow in the top lined with ferns and twigs and containing up to 25 grapefruit-size eggs. They belonged to the Late Cretaceous hadrosaur *Maiasaura*, or "good mother lizard."

Growing families

The biggest dinosaur eggs are only the size of soccer balls, and most are much smaller. This means that dinosaurs grew very fast. The *Maiasaura* young found in Montana were around 18 in (46 cm) long when they hatched but doubled their size within five months. During this time, they were fed by their parents. After this, they grew faster, reaching around 12 ft (3.6 m) in one year and full adult size of 23 ft (7 m) within seven years.

Maiasaura adults seem to have gathered food for their young.

The infants fed in the nest on leaves and fruit brought by their parents, who also defended them.

Saltasaurus

This big plant eater was one of a group of sauropods known as the titanosaurs, which appeared in the Late Jurassic and flourished until the end of the Cretaceous. Judging from fragmentary remains, some were truly titanic, with *Argentinosaurus* possibly growing to more than 100 ft (30 m) long. *Saltasaurus* was much smaller, but it is intriguing because its skin was studded with defensive bony plates.

The titanosaurs were the last of a group of sauropods called the macronarians, or "big noses." They had huge nose openings near the tops of their skulls, but these were probably filled by fleshy nasal cavities leading to normal nostrils.

The titanosaur eggs found in Argentina were roughly spherical, and some were found to contain the fossils of baby saltasaurids. When they hatched, these babies would have been tiny compared to their parents, so it is likely that the adults defended them from danger while they were young.

FOSSIL FINDS: Argentina

FAST FACTS

NAME MEANS:
"lizard from Salta"
DATE: 70–65 mya

DIET: Herbivore

TRIASSIC	JURASSIC	CRETACEOUS	
251 MYA	199	145	65 MYA

LENGTH: 39 ft (12 m)

Although *Saltasaurus* had the body plan of a typical sauropod, its neck was shorter than many.

Nesting site

In 1997, a vast titanosaur nesting ground was discovered in Patagonia, Argentina. It contained the remains of thousands of eggs, each around 6 in (15 cm) across. It is likely that they were *Saltasaurus* eggs. Several hundred females seem to have dug holes, laid their eggs, and then buried them under soil and vegetation.

We do not know what the teeth of *Saltasaurus* were like, but closely related animals had pencil-shaped teeth adapted for pulling leaves off twigs.

Success story

Until quite recently, scientists thought that the sauropods had all but died out in the Cretaceous. But while these giant plant eaters may have declined in North America, titanosaurs were a spectacular success in other parts of the world, right up until the end of the Mesozoic.

The body armor consisted of flat scutes of bone and horny keratin embedded in the skin of the neck, back, and tail.

The legs were massive and pillarlike to support the animal's weight. It had stumpy front feet, with no separate toes. Each back foot had five toes.

Quetzalcoatlus

The Late Cretaceous *Quetzalcoatlus* was one of the biggest of the pterosaurs—a giant of the skies with a wingspan of up to 36 ft (11 m). It could have weighed around 530 lb (240 kg), which is 20 times as much as the heaviest modern flying birds. It is difficult to see how it got airborne, and it may have spent most of its time hunting on the ground. Despite this, it was clearly well adapted for both active flight and soaring like a condor.

The very long beak was like that of a huge bird, with no teeth. The animal seems to have gripped its prey with the sharp beak edges before swallowing its meal.

This colossal creature could have easily caught and eaten small dinosaurs like this baby sauropod. It seems to have hunted mostly on the ground rather than flying down and seizing prey from the air.

The neck skeleton was made up of bones that were tightly linked together. So *Quetzalcoatlus* would have had a stiff, straight neck. Despite this, it was able to pick prey off the ground.

Like many of its relatives, known as azhdarchids, *Quetzalcoatlus* had a big, long-beaked skull topped with an impressive crest. The crest was made of bone sheathed with soft tissue and was probably vividly colored.

The huge wings were membranes of skin reinforced with tough protein fibers, as in all pterosaurs. They were broad, like those of birds that soar on rising air currents.

FAST FACTS

NAME MEANS:
Named after the Aztec god Quezalcoatl

DATE: 70–65 mya

TRIASSIC	JURASSIC	CRETACEOUS	
251 MYA	199	145	65 MYA

WINGSPAN: 36 ft (11 m)

FOSSIL FINDS: North America

DIET: Carnivore

Death stalker

Scientists used to think that *Quetzalcoatlus* and its giant relatives were fish-eaters. They imagined them soaring over the oceans to snatch fish from the surface. But careful studies of its bones indicate that it was well adapted for walking on dry land, so it is now thought that it soared mostly on warm air currents rising off the land, watching for prey such as small dinosaurs. It would then land to stalk its victims—behaving more like a giant stork than a fish-eating sea bird.

When it was foraging on the ground, *Quetzalcoatlus* would have folded its wingtips up and out of the way.

As well as supporting the wings, the front limbs were equipped with fingers that were adapted to support the animal's weight. This would have enabled it to walk on all fours, and it almost certainly did this whenever it was on the ground.

The warm-blooded body would have been covered with fur for insulation. Although heavy by the standards of modern birds, *Quetzalcoatlus* was very light for its size.

Amazing teeth
The teeth were stacked in columns, so as each tooth wore away, it was replaced from below. Altogether, *Edmontosaurus* had more than 1,000 teeth, but only those at the top of each column were in use.

The skull had huge nostril cavities. These may have contained inflatable sacs that made the animal's calls louder.

The big, broad body contained a large digestive system for processing the animal's food. Some of its fossil remains include pine needles, twigs, seeds, and fruit, but we cannot be sure if they were its normal diet.

Edmontosaurus

This very large duck-billed hadrosaur was one of the most successful plant eaters of the Late Cretaceous, especially in North America. It was highly evolved for gathering and processing vegetation, with hundreds of teeth to grind its tough food to a pulp. In turn, it was the favored prey of the most powerful land predators that have ever lived.

Edmontosaurus had long jaws that broadened out at the end. They were tipped with a wide, deep beak of horny tissue for harvesting vegetation, which it chewed up with its batteries of cheek teeth.

FAST FACTS

FOSSIL FINDS: North America

DIET: Herbivore

NAME MEANS:
"Edmonton lizard"
DATE: 70–65 mya

TRIASSIC	JURASSIC	CRETACEOUS	
251 MYA	199	145	65 MYA

LENGTH: 43 ft (13 m)

The back legs were a lot longer and more heavily built than the front ones. But despite this, the animal almost certainly stood on all fours most of the time.

Tyrannosaur prey
Judging from the many skeletons that have been found together, *Edmontosaurus* lived in large herds. As some animals fed, others would use their excellent all-around vision to watch for danger. Even so, many fell prey to hunters. Some skeletons have partly healed injuries that seem to have been inflicted by the teeth of *Tyrannosaurus*.

Its eyes were aimed farther forward than those of other theropods. This gave *Tyrannosaurus* better binocular vision so that it could see well in 3-D, judge distances, and accurately target its prey. Studies of its skull indicate that its brain was very well equipped for processing visual data.

Tyrannosaurus

The most famous of all dinosaurs was one of the most formidable carnivores of the entire Mesozoic era. It was a highly specialized heavyweight hunter, with huge, immensely strong teeth and incredibly powerful jaws. They would have given it the ability to kill and eat virtually any animal it ran into. With no serious enemies of any type, it dominated its habitat as the top predator. So it is not surprising that the only recognized species is called *Tyrannosaurus rex*—the king of the tyrant lizards.

The teeth of most theropods were knife-edged blades, but *Tyrannosaurus* had huge pointed spikes. These were much stronger, enabling it to bite straight through bone. If it broke any teeth, they were soon replaced by new ones.

The arms were tiny, with just two clawed fingers on each hand. They were too short to reach the animal's mouth or even touch each other and could not have been much help while hunting.

Lethal bite

The extremely powerful jaws and sharp, stout teeth of *Tyrannosaurus* were adapted for biting straight through flesh and bone to inflict terrible injuries. This was almost certainly its main tactic—charging in and taking a huge bite that would either cripple its prey or make it die from shock or massive blood loss. It would then rip its victim apart, gulping down great chunks of meat and even bone.

Tyrannosaurus stood with its body roughly horizontal and its long, heavy tail held out stiffly to balance its head and body at the hips. This stance made it very agile for its size.

FAST FACTS

FOSSIL FINDS: North America

NAME MEANS:
"tyrant lizard"
DATE: 70–65 mya

TRIASSIC	JURASSIC	CRETACEOUS	
251 MYA	199	145	65 MYA

DIET: Carnivore

LENGTH: 39 ft (12 m)

The long hind legs had massively muscled thighs but relatively slender ankles and feet. This is typical of a fast-moving animal, so it is likely that Tyrannosaurus could run very fast.

This Triceratops would have been typical prey. Triceratops bones have been found with deep holes and scratches that exactly match the size and spacing of Tyrannosaurus teeth.

End of an era

Tyrannosaurus was one of several very similar tyrannosaurids that preyed on the plant eaters of the Late Cretaceous. They all had the same basic build, with tiny arms but massive skulls and teeth. Yet Tyrannosaurus itself was the biggest. It was also one of the last—a victim of the mass extinction that ended the Mesozoic era 65 million years ago, eliminating the most spectacular animals that have ever walked on Earth.

Glossary

AMMONITE A marine mollusk with a coiled shell and octopuslike tentacles that was common in the Mesozoic era.

AMPHIBIAN A vertebrate animal such as a frog that usually starts life in water as a tadpole but turns into an air-breathing adult that lives at least partly on land.

ANKYLOSAUR One of the main types of ornithischian dinosaurs with a body that was covered with bony armor.

ARCHOSAUR A group of reptiles that includes crocodilians, pterosaurs, dinosaurs, and birds.

ARID Describes a very dry climate or place.

ASTEROID A large rocky object in orbit around the Sun—bigger than a meteor but smaller than a planet.

BACTERIA Microscopic organisms with a simple single-celled structure. Some types live in the digestive systems of animals.

BINOCULAR VISION Seeing a scene or object with two eyes. This enables an animal to see in depth, or 3-D.

BIRD A feathered dinosaur that is able to fly or is descended from flying ancestors.

BREASTBONE The bone in the middle of the chest, which is enlarged in birds.

BREEDING Males and females coming together to produce eggs and/or young.

BREEDING COLONIES Large groups of animals that gather to breed in one place, usually for mutual defense.

BROODING Keeping young animals warm using body heat and feathers. Sometimes used to describe keeping eggs warm.

BROWSE To feed on leaves gathered from trees or bushes.

CAMOUFLAGE A disguise that helps an animal blend in with its surroundings.

CANINES The long, pointed teeth of meat-eating mammals such as dogs and cats.

CARNIVORE Any animal that specializes in eating meat.

CARNOSAUR A type of large, powerful meat-eating theropod that appeared in the Jurassic period.

CARRION Meat obtained from the remains of dead animals.

CARTILAGE The flexible gristle that forms the nonbony parts of an animal's skeleton.

CENOZOIC Literally "new animal life," the era of time that followed the age of dinosaurs (the Mesozoic). It began 65 million years ago and extends up to the present.

CERATOPSIAN A horned dinosaur with a large neck frill, such as *Triceratops*.

CHEEK TEETH The teeth in the sides of the mouth that plant eaters use for chewing their food. Meat eaters rarely chew.

CLUB MOSS A primitive plant with scalelike leaves and spores instead of seeds.

COELUROSAUR An advanced type of theropod that includes tyrannosaurids and maniraptorans.

COLD-BLOODED Refers to a type of animal that relies on the temperature of its surroundings to warm its body enough in order for it to become active.

CONIFER A plant—usually a tall tree such as a pine—that carries its seeds in scaly cones.

CONTOUR FEATHERS The small, stiff feathers that cover a bird's body and help protect it from damage.

COPROLITES Fossilized animal droppings that often contain food fragments.

COURTSHIP Behavior designed to encourage mating, often involving calling and displays of fine plumage.

CRANIUM The domed top of the skull enclosing the brain.

CRETACEOUS The third period of the Mesozoic era, or "age of dinosaurs," which began 145 million years ago and ended 65 million years ago.

CROCODILIANS Modern crocodiles and alligators and their close fossil relatives.

CROCODYLOMORPHS The archosaur group that includes crocodilians and similar animals that lived in the Mesozoic.

CRUROTARSAN A major archosaur group that includes crocodylomorphs as well as various other groups, but not dinosaurs or pterosaurs. Most crurotarsan groups were unique to the Triassic.

CYCAD A tropical or subtropical plant that bears its seeds in large cones but has a crown of foliage like a tree fern or palm.

DIGESTION The breakdown of food into simpler substances that can be absorbed and used by an animal's body.

DIGITIGRADE Walking or standing on the toes rather than on the sole of the foot.

DINOSAUR One of a large, successful group of reptiles that supported their weight off the ground and probably had a warm-blooded physiology.

DIPLODOCID A member of the dinosaur family that included the giant long-necked sauropod *Diplodocus*.

DISPLAY In animals, a demonstration of fitness or strength, usually designed to impress a rival or potential mate. Some displays can be designed to discourage or distract possible predators.

DOWN FEATHERS Soft, fluffy feathers that, in birds, are purely to keep them warm.

DROMEOSAUR A type of theropod dinosaur with long, clawed arms and a specialized "killer claw" on each foot. They include *Deinonychus* and *Velociraptor*.

EROSION Wearing away, usually by natural forces such as frost or rain or waves on the seashore.

EXTINCT Having died out completely and permanently. An extinct species has no living individuals and is gone forever.

FERMENTATION A process in which food or similar material is broken down into simpler substances without involving air.

FILAMENTS Thin, hairlike structures.

FLASH FLOOD A flood that rises very quickly after a rainstorm and may form a powerful torrent.

FLIGHT FEATHERS The long, stiff feathers that grow from the back of a bird's wing and form most of its area.

FLIGHT MUSCLES The big breast muscles that power the wings of a bird or pterosaur.

FOSSIL The remains or traces of any living thing that survive the normal processes of decay or destruction and that are often preserved by being turned to stone.

GINKGO One of a group of nonflowering plants that grows into a tall tree with more or less triangular leaves.

GIZZARD A thick-walled part of the digestive system of some animals in which food is mashed up by muscular action.

HABITAT The environment in which an animal (or any living thing) lives.

HADROSAUR An advanced type of ornithopod dinosaur with a ducklike bill and batteries of chewing teeth.

HERBIVORE An animal that eats plants.

HORNY Made of keratin, the substance that forms the outer layers of animal horns, bird beaks, claws, fingernails, scales, and hair.

HORSETAIL A primitive type of plant that produces spores instead of seeds and has threadlike leaves that grow from the stem in rings or whorls.

ICHTHYOSAUR One of a group of dolphinlike marine reptiles that was very common in the early Mesozoic era.

IGUANODONT An advanced ornithopod dinosaur with a toothless beak at the front of its jaws, but chewing teeth at the back.

INCUBATE To keep eggs warm so that they develop and hatch.

INSULATION In animals, anything that helps stop heat from escaping from the body, such as fat, fur, or feathers.

INVERTEBRATE An animal without a vertebral column (backbone).

IRIDESCENT The glittering rainbow effect created by the way the microscopic structure of an object such as a feather reflects and scatters light.

JURASSIC The second period of the Mesozoic era, or "age of dinosaurs," which began 199 million years ago and ended 145 million years ago.

KEEL BONE The enlarged, deepened breastbone of a bird that is well adapted for flight. It anchors the large flight muscles.

KERATIN A tough structural protein found in hair, feathers, scales, claws, and horns.

LAGOON An area of shallow water that has been cut off from the sea.

Hunters like *Compsognathus* would also eat dead meat, or **carrion**.

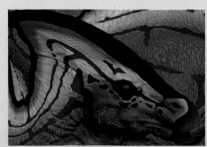
The pterosaur *Pterodactylus* needed big **flight muscles** to get airborne.

Parasaurolophus was an unusually long-crested type of **hadrosaur.**

The Late Cretaceous *Edmontosaurus* was a highly specialized **herbivore**.

MAMMAL One of a group of warm-blooded, often hairy vertebrates that feed their young on milk supplied by the female.

MANIRAPTORAN Literally "hand grabber"—an advanced type of theropod with powerful arms and claws, which includes birds as well as dromeosaurs and oviraptorosaurs.

MARGINOCEPHALIAN A major group of ornithischians that consisted of the horned dinosaurs (ceratopsians) and bone heads (pachycephalosaurs).

MEMBRANE A thin, flexible, often elastic sheet of a material such as skin.

MESOZOIC Literally "middle animal life," the era of time that includes the age of dinosaurs. It began 251 million years ago and ended 65 million years ago.

MIGRATION The regular, often yearly roundtrip that an animal makes in search of feeding areas or breeding sites.

NEOGENE The period of time that forms the second and most recent period of the Cenozoic era. It began 23 million years ago and extends up to the present.

NEURAL SPINES Bony projections that extend upward from the vertebrae—the bones that form the backbone.

NODOSAURID One of a family of ankylosaurs that did not have a heavy club on the end of its tail.

NUTRIENTS Substances that living things need to build their tissues.

OMNIVORE An animal that has a broad diet, including animal and plant material.

ORNITHISCHIAN A member of the order Ornithischia, one of the two primary types of dinosaurs (the other is the order Saurischia).

ORNITHOPOD One of the three main groups of ornithischian dinosaurs.

OVIRAPTORID One of a family of theropod dinosaurs with beaks and feathered arms, named after *Oviraptor*.

PACHYCEPHALOSAUR A type of ornithischian dinosaur with a very thick skull, including *Pachycephalosaurus*.

PALEOGENE The period of time that formed the first period of the Cenozoic era. It began 65 million years ago and ended 23 million years ago.

PALEOZOIC Literally "ancient animal life," the era of time that preceded the age of dinosaurs (the Mesozoic). It began 542 million years ago and ended 251 million years ago.

PELVIC Having to do with the pelvis, the skeletal structure that the upper leg bones are attached to at the hips.

PHYSIOLOGY The mechanical, physical, and chemical functions of a living thing.

PLACODONT A turtlelike marine reptile that lived in the Triassic period.

PLESIOSAUR One of a group of typically long-necked marine reptiles with four roughly equal-size flippers that lived throughout the Mesozoic era.

PLIOSAUR A type of plesiosaur (see above) with a shorter neck, larger head and jaws, and a more predatory lifestyle.

POLLEN Tiny grains produced by flowers to fertilize other flowers so they set seed.

PREDATOR An animal that hunts and kills other animals (prey) for food.

PREY An animal that is killed and eaten by another animal (a predator).

PROSAUROPOD An early, mostly plant-eating saurischian dinosaur, ancestral to the giant long-necked sauropods.

PROTEIN A complex substance that a living thing makes out of simpler nutrients and uses to form its tissues.

PROTOFEATHERS Hairlike structures evolved by dinosaurs for insulation, which later evolved into recognizable feathers.

PTERODACTYLOID An advanced type of pterosaur (see below) with a short tail, named after *Pterodactylus*.

PTEROSAUR A flying reptile with batlike wings supported by the bones of a single very elongated finger.

REPTILE A vertebrate animal belonging to the class Reptilia. Modern reptiles are cold-blooded scaly animals that include snakes, lizards, tortoises, and crocodiles, but warm-blooded pterosaurs and dinosaurs are also classified as reptiles.

SAURISCHIAN A member of the order Saurischia, one of the two primary types of dinosaurs (the other is the order Ornithischia).

SAUROPOD One of a group of giant long-necked, four-footed plant-eating saurischian dinosaurs that appeared in the Late Triassic and survived until the end of the Mesozoic era.

SAUROPODOMORPH One of the two main groups of saurischian dinosaurs, which included the sauropods (see above).

SCAVENGER An animal that lives on the remains of dead animals and other scraps.

SCUTE A tough, often protective plate embedded in the skin, with a bony base and a covering of scaly keratin.

SEDIMENT Solid particles such as sand, silt, or mud that have settled on the seabed or elsewhere. They may harden to form sedimentary rock.

SERRATED Sawtoothed, like a steak knife.

SOARING A form of flight that, over land, involves circling on rising currents of warm air on outspread wings, like a vulture.

SPECIES The basic unit of classification of living organisms. Members of a species look like one another and can reproduce by pairing with one another, but not with members of other species.

SPINOSAUR A type of large, long-snouted theropod dinosaur that had crocodile-like teeth and jaws, adapted for eating fish.

STAMINA The quality needed to stay active for long periods of time instead of short bursts.

STEGOSAUR A type of ornithischian dinosaur with rows of plates and/or spines extending down its back, named after *Stegosaurus*.

STEREOSCOPIC VISION See binocular vision.

SUPERCONTINENT An ancient landmass, such as Pangaea, that is much bigger than any modern continent.

SYNAPSID One of a group of vertebrate animals that includes mammals and their ancestors.

TEMPERATE A climate that is neither very hot nor very cold.

TENDON A strong, slightly elastic cordlike structure in the body that attaches muscles to bones or bones to one another.

TERRITORY The part of an animal's habitat that it defends from rival animals, usually of its own species.

TETANURAN One of a group of advanced stiff-tailed theropod dinosaurs, which included carnosaurs, tyrannosaurs, and maniraptorans.

TETRAPOD A four-limbed vertebrate or any vertebrate with four-limbed ancestors. In practice, all vertebrates except fish.

THERIZINOSAUROID One of a group of plant-eating, large-clawed theropods, named after *Therizinosaurus*.

THEROPOD One of the two main groups of saurischian dinosaurs, which were mostly two-footed meat eaters.

THYREOPHORAN One of the three main groups of ornithischian dinosaurs, which included the plated stegosaurs and armored ankylosaurs.

TITANOSAUR A late-evolving type of sauropod dinosaur that survived until the end of the Mesozoic era.

TRIASSIC The first period of the Mesozoic era, or "age of dinosaurs," which began 251 million years ago and ended 199 million years ago.

TYRANNOSAUR A term that is sometimes used for tyrannosaurids.

TYRANNOSAURID One of a family of coelurosaurs with very short arms and two-fingered hands, named after the big, powerful *Tyrannosaurus*.

TYRANNOSAUROID A theropod that belongs to the same group as tyrannosaurids and their primitive relatives.

VANE A lightweight sheet of material that responds to air pressure, like a weathervane.

VERTEBRAE The bones that make up the backbone of an animal such as a dinosaur, bird, or mammal.

VERTEBRATE An animal with a vertebral column (backbone) made of a long, flexible chain of vertebrae.

WARM-BLOODED Refers to an animal that uses internal chemical reactions to keep its body constantly warm, no matter whether its surroundings are hot or cold.

The plant-eating *Lesothosaurus* was an early beaked **ornithischian**.

Isanosaurus was one of the earliest four-footed plant-eating **sauropods**.

Coelophysis was a hunter with many knife-like teeth—a typical **theropod**.

The mighty *Tyrannosaurus rex* is the best-known **tyrannosaurid**.

Index

Acknowledgments

Dorling Kindersley would like to thank
Stephanie Pliakas for proofreading and Americanization, Jackie Brind for the index, and Stefan Podhorodecki for design assistance.

The publisher would like to thank the following for their kind permission to reproduce their photographs:
(Key: a-above; b-below/bottom; c-center; f-far; l-left; r-right; t-top)

5 Corbis: Owen Franken (fcrb/*Citipati* background); Alan Traeger (crb/*Saltasaurus* background). **6** Dorling Kindersley: Richard Hammond modelmaker/Oxford University Museum of Natural History (cb). **6–7** Corbis: Louie Psihoyos (tc). **7** Science Photo Library: Mauricio Anton (bc). **8** Getty Images: Whit Richardson/Aurora (tr). **9** Dorling Kindersley: Senckenberg Forschungsinstitut und Naturmuseum, Frankfurt (tr); Jerry Young (tl). Getty Images: DAJ (bl/background of illustration). **10** Dorling Kindersley: Robert L. Braun modelmaker (clb/*Stegosaurus*). **11** Science Photo Library: Roger Harris (tl). **12** Corbis: Owaki-Kulla (clb). **12–13** Plate Tectonic and Paleogeographic Maps by C. R. Scotese, © 2007, PALEOMAP Project (www.scotese.com): (c). **13** Dorling Kindersley: Natural History Museum, London (tl). Getty Images: De Agostini Picture Library (bl). **14–15** Dorling Kindersley: David Peart (background). **16–17** Corbis: Jon Spark (background). **18–19** Corbis: Randall Levensaler.

Photography/Aurora Photos (background). **21** Ardea: François Gohier (tl). Getty Images: Robert Postma (cr). **24–25** Corbis: Nobuaki Sumida/amanaimages (background). **26–27** Corbis: Mark A. Johnson (water and sky background). **28–29** Corbis: Jon Spark (desert background). **30** Science Photo Library: Simon Fraser (clb). **30–31** Plate Tectonic and Paleogeographic Maps by C. R. Scotese, © 2007, PALEOMAP Project (www.scotese.com): (c). **32–33** Corbis: Paul A. Souders (background). **34–35** Corbis: Mark A. Johnson (background). **36** Dorling Kindersley: American Museum of Natural History (cra); Luis Rey modelmaker (br). **37** Ardea: Peter J. Green (clb). Getty Images: Philip and Karen Smith (t/background of illustration). **38–39** Corbis: Radius Images (b/fern background); Kevin Schafer (t/forest background). **40–41** Getty Images: (background). **42–43** Getty Images: Oliver Strewe (background). **44–45** Getty Images: Siri Stafford (background). **47** Bailey Archive, Denver Museum of Nature & Science: (crb). **48–49** Getty Images: Holger Spiering (background). **50–51** Corbis: J. Joyce/zefa (desert background). **52–53** Getty Images: DAJ (background). **54** The Natural History Museum, London: Anness Publishing (br). **55** Getty Images: O. Louis Mazzatenta/National Geographic (bl); Spencer Platt (tl); Peter Schouten: (cra). **56–57** Corbis: Moodboard (background). **58–59** Corbis: Mitsushi Okada/amanaimages (sky background). **60** Getty Images: TG Stock/Tim Graham Photo Library (clb). **60–61**

Plate Tectonic and Paleogeographic Maps by C. R. Scotese, © 2007, PALEOMAP Project (www.scotese.com): (c). **61** Carl Buell: (bl). **62–63** Alamy Images: Eric Nathan (background). **64–65** Getty Images: Stockbyte (background). **66–67** Corbis: Nick Rains (background). **68–69** Getty Images: Philip and Karen Smith (background). **70** StoneCompany.com, Inc.: (tr). **71** Dorling Kindersley: Senckenberg Forschungsinstitut und Naturmuseum, Frankfurt (t). The Natural History Museum, London: Geological Museum of China (bl). Nobumichi Tamura: (br). **72–73** Corbis: Owen Franken (background). **77** Mathew J. Wedel: (tc). **78–79** Photolibrary: Peter Lilja (background). **80–81** Corbis: Inspirestock (background). **82–83** Corbis: Radius Images (background). **84** Department of the Environment, Water, Heritage and the Arts, Australia: Mark Mohell (tr). Museum of the Rockies: (bl/fossilized *Troodon* egg). **85** Corbis: Louie Psihoyos (tl). **86–87** Corbis: Alan Traeger (background). **88–89** Getty Images: Bob O'Connor (background). **90–91** Getty Images: Panoramic Images (background). **92–93** Getty Images: Willard Clay/Photographer's Choice (background). **94** Corbis: Mitsushi Okada/amanaimages (background of illustration). Getty Images: DAJ (bl/background of illustration). **95** Corbis: Randall Levensaler Photography/Aurora Photos (br/background of illustration); Jon Spark (bl/background of illustration). Getty Images: Willard Clay/Photographer's Choice (fbr/background of illustration).

Plate Tectonic and Paleogeographic Maps by C. R. Scotese, © 2007, PALEOMAP Project (www.scotese.com): (c). **61** Carl Buell: (bl). **62–63**

All other images © Dorling Kindersley
For further information see:
www.dkimages.com

Allosaurus